THE OTHER SIDE OF FEAR

BY:

BARBARA BECK

CONTENTS

ACKNOWLEDGEMENTS

I Am Grateful...

To Jesus: My life has been one continuous miracle because of you, my Lord. I pray the words on these pages somehow glorify your holy name and bring honor to the Kingdom.

To my friends and family who wouldn't let me quit: You know who you are. God bless you for helping me find the strength and the courage to see this book through.

To all the people who said it couldn't be done: You know who you are, as well. God bless you, also, for causing me to dig into a deeper faith.

To LWCC in Forest Park, Illinois, and the Dean of the School of Ministry: "Thank you" could never be enough to convey the countless ways you continue to influence my life. I would not have written this book, had you not chosen to stand for the truth of Jesus, to show the world the Kingdom inside of us, and the power thereof.

ENDORSEMENTS

'The Other Side of Fear is written for such a time as this.

Barbara Beck's heart for people shines through every word she writes as she recounts the milestones in her own journey to the Triune God.

Barbara's writing is sensitive and encouraging. Her passion for the gifts of the Holy Spirit is revealed as she shares true, life-changing events.

As a pastor and a lifetime professional counselor, she reveals her heart so that each individual may come to walk in the very fullness of the Kingdom of God. She highlights God's promises from His Word in an engaging and approachable way.

If you are looking for more, this is the book for you. Barbara's words ring true and leave me wanting more . . . every single time.

Enjoy!'

Clarence Larsen, Author
SwordLight and Chronicles of Armor

"In this uplifting, inspirational memoir about finding Jesus, Barbara shares how the unknown can build a wall of fear only God can tear down. A must read for anyone who is searching for the truth."

Heidi Thomas, Award-winning Author
Cowgirls Dreams, American Dream, and Rescue

"This book captured my attention from beginning to end. It helped me realize that when I think I hear God's voice, I really do. Barbara helped me feel less afraid of my true, supernatural, Kingdom identity."

Diana Robinson, Administrator
Grace Church, Chino Valley, AZ

PREFACE

Nobody ever taught me that God is a supernatural, triune God.

No one, not even one person in His church, ever told me that my life just might be a life filled with prophecy.

I didn't even know what prophecy was until recently; until I finally reached the point in my journey where I was sick and tired of being afraid.

That's when He came to me.

That's when Jesus talked to me and gave me the courage to write everything down for Him. All the unusual experiences I've had in life, the pain, the feelings of isolation, the joy, the fear, the guilt of choosing Him over my family; the Lord said to write and tell you: you are never alone. God keeps His Word.

As we approach Jesus' return, it's not enough that we are in Him, and He in us. It's time to live as He lived, to do what He did, and more.

This book is written to show you what life may be like when it's filled with the supernatural love and power of our living God.

Beginning at age three, it has for me been one continuous series of unusual events that could only have been orchestrated by Him.

As a believer, I am very much for Christ's church. I am honored to be an important part of His body. However, not discussing the truth of the miraculous Jesus in our lives, nor encouraging us to do what He has done, has been a very serious disservice to Him.

How could the church, in general, overlook the major theme of the Bible?

The body of Christ needs to come to an understanding of prophecy.

God calls people out. In fact, He's been known to do it way before we might know anything about His true nature. In the book of Isaiah, the Bible says:

"It shall come to pass That before they call, I will answer
And while they are still speaking, I will hear"
(Isaiah 64:24 NKJV).

Yes, God's ways are not like our ways at all, and His thoughts not our thoughts.

Ignorance of the truth of our Lord cost me years. Don't let it cost you, as well.

I look forward to looking back with you, dear readers, and sharing with you what it was like to be different, i.e., the tears, the fear, as well as the incomprehensible joy that finally came with learning to trust Jesus above all else.

People who read this book will gain confidence; confidence in their own unique spiritual gifts, and confidence in the miraculous life of perfect love for which we've been created.

My purpose?

That those who read through this book will journey with me, hand in hand, from wherever they are at... to the other side of fear.

In His Love,
Barbara

INTRODUCTION

I sat across the table from the woman, and hoped the skills I'd acquired as a counselor would help her. I wasn't so sure, though.

We needed more.

We needed Jesus.

We needed Him right now.

Silently, I prayed.

The worn-out room around us faded into the background and offered up a quiet comfort as we both faced what would be a difficult conversation.

Her flaxen-colored hair hung past her shoulders and all but covered her face as she stared down at her lap. She wouldn't look at me, which led me to guess that violence and shame were close companions in this woman's life.

The afternoon sun peeked through the plastic blinds on the tall window beside us. Small beams of light danced over the nicks and scars on the ancient wooden tabletop. Those scars were obvious. Hers were not.

In a barely audible voice, while still looking down at her lap, the woman finally spoke. Not only had a so-called "family friend" raped her years ago, but her stepfather had watched. She also shared that her husband had recently physically abused her. A woman of battered faith, filled with deep rage, she focused intently on the hands folded on her lap.

"I'm afraid of living," she whispered.

"What do you mean?" I sat back in the hard, wooden chair and looked at her face. I assumed she was afraid of living because of the horror she had experienced in life.

So, I waited and hoped she would look up at me.
It was then that she lifted her head and stared back at me for what seemed like forever. She did not blink. Clear, intelligent blue eyes bore right into my own, while she decided if she could truly trust me with her thoughts.

Finally, she spoke. "Sometimes I sense angels. I can see demons in people and feel the presence of angels. *That* is why I am afraid of living. I am like a little girl inside. I am innocent. Do you think I'm crazy?"

As I look back, God could not have given me a clearer confirmation of the need for this book.

This grown woman, once married to a pastor, had never been esteemed, let alone mentored in God's spiritual gifts. Instead, she'd come to know fear: fear of herself, fear of Jesus, fear of

His gifts, and fear of our triune God. She was never taught that the fear talked about in the Bible often means "awe," "respect," or "reverence," not holy terror.

Our triune God is not out to hurt us.

In fact, I believe, as the body of Christ, we are in a season that calls us to be confident, without a doubt, of who we are in Him. It is imperative we know Him in His gifts for us, that we become true miraculous vessels as we experience the fullness of the Word.

So, I write. This is a book about what it's like to live with the unseen, supernatural power of God, to be gloriously gifted with eyes that truly see and ears that hear.

Just as salvation is freely given to anyone who wants it, so is a miraculous, supernatural life. We are meant to experience heaven on earth, not feel afraid.

We are meant to know God in His gifts; to know one another in all of His gifts, and to embrace all of them.

This book is for people who relate to the woman who sat across from me that day. Meeting her was a turning point in both of our lives.

She was frightened by the gifts God had given to her, gifts that guided and often protected her.

She was frightened of herself. In fact, she thought she was crazy.

This battered woman did not know that to allow God to be God in our lives, and delight in His ways means to live in the supernatural power of love.

Why would God's love, greater than we can ever imagine, frighten people? Why would a life filled with blatant signs, wonders, and miracles cause people to run out the back door?

Dear readers, life with Jesus is beautiful and daunting. It is as wondrous as a midnight sky full of twinkling stars. I write and share my experiences with you to show you there's nothing to fear, and to instead inspire you and bring you hope.

I pray these pages spark passion in you. As I look back to share my life experiences with you, I pray you will feel encouraged to step out and live your dreams; that my words shower you with understanding and courage.

All events in this book are true, though I've changed all names and descriptions of various locations. This has been done out of respect for everyone's privacy.

Stand tall, my friends. Life with our triune God is better than you could ever imagine. What may seem weird or like craziness to you could in truth turn out to be a treasure, a precious, priceless gift of invitation from almighty God, Himself.

I pray you will accept it and read on.

PROLOGUE

"Also I say to you, whoever confesses Me before men him the Son of Man also will confess before the angels of God" (Luke 12:8 NKJV).

There were only a few weeks left until Christmas.

The sun had long gone down, and the air held a definite chill. Lately, I'd noticed a slight bite to the cold. That told me we were headed for temperatures in the teens, maybe even the single digits.

I was buried on my couch underneath a thick, soft throw painted with Christmas trees. If I recall correctly, the only parts of me that showed were my eyes, nose, and mouth.

Relaxed while enjoying a movie on TV, I suddenly heard the Lord whisper in my heart. "There are huge warriors all around the outside of this building."

Startled by the clarity of Jesus' voice, I quickly sat up on the couch.

"Huh? Why?" I spoke out loud.

"You're never alone." Jesus' voice was so soft and gentle, my heart melted, and tears filled my eyes.

"Thank you," I whispered. "You're amazing, and I adore you."

Shifting on the couch, I turned my attention to the lights on my Christmas tree. This time of the year had challenged me for a long time. I loved Christmas but missed Michael something awful. The love of my life, he'd been gone for many years. Life without him was hard.

For some reason, I felt more lonely than usual this year, and I'd written to God about it. For the first time ever, I asked Him for specific miracles, wanting sincerely to feel joy again during this holiday season.

So that night, I surmised that Jesus knew all about my letter, seeing as how I'd asked for things in His name.

I figured He also was aware I was having trouble this season finding the right angel for my Christmas tree. Covid19 had been rampant, and there was a definite shortage of holiday decorations everywhere.

I sat back on the couch and smiled. Jesus knew I hadn't been able to find an angel for my tree, and he knew I was struggling. So, it only made sense that He sent me God's heavenly hosts to cheer me up. How precious is that?

Ready to watch the rest of the movie, I thanked Jesus out loud. As I did, I felt a nudge from Spirit in my heart. Hmm, I guess He wasn't done wanting my attention.

"Yes, Lord?" And with that, the doorbell rang, scaring the wits out of me.

I jumped up and quickly unwrapped myself from the cozy throw. I shivered my way over to the heavy black sweater hanging on the back of the dining room chair. I stuck my arms in it, and quickly stuffed my feet into a pair of nearby slippers. Then I shuffled to the front door.

I pulled it open, and lo and behold, on the other side stood my neighbors! Maggie, John, and their tiny dog, Sweetpea, smiled at me as I said hello and quickly ushered them in, out of the cold.

"I saw this and thought of you," Maggie explained as she held out a medium size package wrapped in bright blue tissue. "Merry Christmas!"

Utterly delighted by this unexpected visit, I took the package from Maggie and looked at her, then at John, then at Sweetpea. A huge grin spread across my face.

"Thank you!" I tore away the tissue.

Immediately, delight turned to shock. I gasped. "Oh my gosh!"

Maggie, John, and Sweetpea looked at me funny. Sweetpea wagged her tail, and squirmed in John's arms, trying to come to me and join in my excitement.

But all I could do was stare at the gift, because in my hand I held the most beautiful glass angel ever made. I'm certain this Christmas tree ornament was one of a kind.

"It just reminded me of you," Maggie said.

I looked at her, needing a few seconds before speaking. I was close to tears, and certain my visitors could tell.

So, I just stood for a few seconds to gather my wits about me. Instead of trying to explain all that had just happened, I focused my attention on my neighbors, scratching Sweetpea between her ears. We chatted cheerfully for a few minutes, wished one another a Merry Christmas, then said our goodbyes.

Dumbfounded, I closed the front door, and immediately walked over to my Christmas tree. I looked up to the top, and for what seemed like forever, I searched.

Finally, I felt my eyes rest upon the perfect tree branch, with the most beautiful colored lights tucked behind it. Very carefully, I hung the angel on the tree.

Reds, greens, and blues danced with excitement behind the delicate glass. I stood for a moment, amazed at Jesus and what He had just done.

"Barbara, tell them. Start with tonight. One of the first steps to receiving a miracle is knowing you are never alone. It's time to let go and tell the others."

"What do you mean I should let go and tell the others? Let go of what?" Surprised by what my heart was hearing, a tear trickled down my left cheek as I responded out loud.

I sat back down on the couch and looked up at the glass angel.

"Good. Let's begin. Get your pen and paper." Though Jesus' voice was within me, he might as well have been shouting from the rooftop.

I wasted no time and did what He asked.

Of course, I had no idea what the Lord was talking about that night. He didn't give me any clues, either. He just proceeded to ask me to share with you my profound, life-long journey to Him.

The thing is though, He wasn't asking me to share the fake story: the one filled with religious cliches that paint the faith-walk as flowery, and rosy, and always full of happiness. Jesus wanted me to tell you the real story of what happened, how alone I felt, and how afraid I'd been most of my life – of Him, and His magnificence.

He tricked me the night my neighbors came to the door. By asking me to write and share with you my experiences for your sake, He has brought me to the other side of fear.

Just as He is about to do for you.

PART ONE:

THE INSIDIOUS
DANCE OF FEAR

CHAPTER 1

IN THE BEGINNING...

There was fire.

The little girl stood on the sidewalk in the middle of town and watched. The office building across the street was so tall, it looked as if the dancing fire reached all the way up to the stars. The orange flames waving like a banner across the nighttime sky mesmerized her.

Oblivious to the fact that she was alone, she watched as the men across the street tried to put the fire out. She wasn't frightened. She wasn't upset at all. She was just there, fascinated by the flames.

The little girl woke abruptly. The dream seemed so real. Startled, she sat upright in the small twin bed tucked into the corner of the room. She rubbed her eyes as they adjusted to the dark, then turned her head to make certain her sister was sleeping in the other bed.

She looked over at the familiar purple quilt with white butterflies on it. It was lumpy. Yes, she could barely make out her sister's head and shoulders. Oh, there was Sleepy Hollow too, their stuffed dog.

Satisfied, the little girl lay back on her pillow and closed her tired eyes. At three years old, she didn't give any further thought to the dream. In fact, for years she never mentioned it. It's as though that night she went back to sleep, and someone took the dream, put it on an attic shelf for safe keeping, and kept it there until the exact time she would need to remember.

You see, I know this because that little girl was me.

God calls us when He calls us, for His plans, as He sees fit. His ways are most definitely not our ways. Personally, I'm most grateful for that.

Reference to fire is prominent throughout the Bible. According to the internet, it is mentioned six hundred and twenty-seven times.

Though the word is defined in a variety of ways, fire in the Bible has been most closely associated with experiencing God. For example, in the book of Exodus fire is used to describe the manifestation of an angel of God, i.e., a burning bush. Later, in the same book, fire is used to describe the glory of God.

But to me, the most intriguing and most relevant reference of fire is the way it's spoken of in the books of Matthew and Acts. It is referenced in conjunction with the Holy Spirit, the manifestation of the third member of the Godhead:

"I indeed baptize you with water unto repentance, but He who is coming after me is mightier than I, whose sandals I am not worthy to carry. He will baptize you with the Holy Spirit and fire" (Matthew 3:11 NKJV).

And further,

"They saw what seemed to be tongues of fire that separated and came to rest on each of them. All of them were filled with the Holy Spirit and began to speak in other tongues as the Spirit enabled them"
(Acts 2:3-4 NKJV).

Perhaps in these instances, fire is an example of two of Noah Webster's 1828 definitions. He refers to it as light, luster, splendor, and that which inflames or irritates the passions.

The dream I had of fire, as vivid now as it was years ago, was a beginning for me of a gifted and unusual life filled with our triune God.

Eventually, after years of preparation, I would recognize the dream for what it was and come to understand the fire inside me for who He is, constantly burning wildly, deep in my heart and soul.

However, as a little girl, I was oblivious. I could have cared less about the dream. My main interests were my toys, especially my dolls.

Life for me consisted of days filled with typical activities like riding my tricycle, blowing bubbles, eating fun, sugary snacks, and trying to catch fireflies as the summer sun went down. Being three years old was perfect.

My family, immediate as well as extended, practiced the Jewish religion on what was called the High Holidays. We went to temple three times a year: on Rosh Hashanah (Jewish New Year), on Passover, and on Yom Kippur (Day of Atonement).

I went to Sunday school and was confirmed. But truthfully? I don't remember much of those times.

My parents worked evenings at their dress shop in town.

That meant that just about every night they were both gone, and a babysitter came to stay with my sister and me.

Now, that's not so unusual. But what is interesting, is that most evenings our sitter, Janice, walked in, hung up her coat, checked on my sister and me, and waited for our parents to leave.

Hmm, once the coast was clear, instead of turning on TV, or playing a game with us, she marched right over to our baby grand piano in the living room, sat down, and played old hymns on our piano. She belted out the Gospel, one song after another, all about Jesus.

What's even more interesting, is that while my sister usually went into another room, I listened and sometimes sang along with Janice. I was at peace, the same kind of peace as when I stood in the dream and watched the fire.

What did it mean?

Fire? Songs of Jesus in our living room?

Could I have unknowingly made Him my Savior through the words of old gospel hymns? Could Janice have known that my sister and I were about to face a family life filled with loss, lies, and deceit? Was it her prayers that ultimately saved us?

Better yet, was Janice an angel?

Regardless of the specific answers to these questions, this kind woman undoubtedly planted seeds of the Kingdom into my heart.

Like a giant ball of multi-colored yarn, God's call on my life began to unravel, all while I was busy being three years old.

CHAPTER 2

HOPE

Years passed by, and life was sort of normal, "sort of" being the operative phrase.

My dad was a buyer of ladies' fashions, and traveled quite a bit, while my mom stayed in town and ran the dress shop.

My sister and I were left most of the time in the care of one of the sweetest women who ever lived. Emma Parks was very much a mom to me. The first day that we all met her, she became part of our family. She changed my life for the better.

The other important event that occurred during that time, was the day I combed the newspaper classifieds, and answered an ad about a litter of puppies. My sister and I wanted a dog, something fierce.

That evening my father took us to look at a litter of pups. Supposedly, they were part collie and part shepherd, not that it mattered to my sister or me. We carefully held each little furball and watched the others as they stumbled and fumbled over their mother. Finally, we picked out Chippie.

No bigger than my hand, Chippie came home with us that evening, and grew to become, without a doubt, my most faithful and dearest friend, ever. The thing is though, he was not a collie or a shepherd. He was a mixture of shepherd and basset hound. Funny looking was an understatement.

But you know what? Chippie was love personified. He was patient, loyal, and true. He allowed me to dress him up in my mother's paisley head scarves, and looking like Grandma Moses, he allowed me to take him for a walk down the street.

Now that's what I call love. I depended on Chippie more than anyone, even Emma Parks.

A few years went by, and before I knew it, I was in high school, a phenomenon all its own. I don't care what anyone says, I've never met a person who wasn't, to some degree, traumatized by high school.

It was my sophomore year. My sister had left for college, and since I didn't need a babysitter anymore, Emma left also. Dad traveled, and Mom worked almost all the time.

So, most days I came home from school to, well, no one. Life had changed drastically without my consent. Chippie and I had many conversations about it during this time.

Back then there weren't any cell phones or computers. There was no social media. There were only three TV stations, and a new burger joint called McDonald's.

It didn't help any that my boyfriend, Bob, had just broken up with me so that he could date "an older woman," or that my best friend had recently found the love of her life. Now she spent most of her free time with him, instead of me.

It wasn't fair. Everyone I thought I could depend on was gone or too busy for me. I felt abandoned, lonely, and confused. I was angry. All I ever really wanted was to have friends, have a boyfriend like all the other girls I knew, be invited to parties, and of course, the prom.

But the Lord had other plans.

It was Tuesday morning. I deliberately walked slowly down the high school hallway because it was the day that Dave Johnson usually passed me by. My dark curls swayed back and forth from behind a pale pink headband. I wore a new red dress and hoped to run into Dave before my next class. Gosh, he was cute. My heart tripped in anticipation.

I purposely took my time meandering down the hall, and that's when I happened to notice a heavy-set girl in wrinkled jeans and a navy pea coat.

As she came closer, I could see pock marks on her face, and her short dark hair looked greasy, as if she hadn't recently bathed. She walked right up to me, then stopped.

"Hi, my name is Hope Danbury."

Oh no!

I gulped. My eyes darted everywhere, as I avoided hers. I had hoped Dave would notice me today and clearly didn't want this rumpled-looking girl messing up my chances.

"Hello." I kept on walking and much to my dismay, Hope changed directions and walked right along with me.

"I had an older sister," she began. "She was a senior here, but last month she committed suicide."

I stopped so abruptly I'm certain I laid rubber on the shiny hallway floor. My jaw dropped as I turned to Hope.

"I … I … I don't know what to say. I'm so sorry," I whispered.

"Do you believe in God?" Hope started walking again. "I do. We were raised Catholic, but now I just believe in Jesus. I don't go to church or anything. Do you believe in heaven?"

I didn't know how to respond. She was asking me about things I rarely thought about, if ever. Totally caught off guard by the whole encounter, I just stared at her.

Finally, I found my voice. "Do you want to go get a milkshake? It's on me." That's all I could think to say.

I never did run into Dave Johnson that day. I was so surprised by Hope and what she shared, I forgot all about him.

The two of us walked to the diner across the street from school and talked for quite a while. It was to be the first of many conversations as well as many milkshakes I shared with Hope.

After high school graduation I floundered. I worked, shopped, and hoped to meet Mr. Right. That's what I was taught to do.

I felt angry, was bored, and plain miserable.

I made mistake after mistake. Rebellion became my middle name. I lived in pursuit of bell bottom jeans and the Beatles' latest album.

Though the Lord had used Hope to nudge me in His direction, to water and bring life to the spiritual seeds He had planted deep in my heart, it would be years before I would understand Him at all.

As little more than a teenager, having grown up basically with a dog and a babysitter, I was clueless.

And having an extended Jewish family didn't help. The name of Jesus was used in vain in our house, if at all. It never dawned on me to consider Him as the Son of God, let alone as my Lord and Savior.

I felt like the proverbial round peg trying desperately to fit into a square hole. When that didn't work, I gave up and tried to be the square peg everyone thought I should be. Clearly, that was a disaster.

It looked like I wasn't ever going to be in the round hole or the square one. What now?

Where did I fit?

As I gave thought to the answer to that question, what came to mind was the day I had asked Hope why she had chosen me in the hall that first day we met.

She claimed she had no idea.

Well, neither did the others.

CHAPTER 3

CURVEBALLS AND HOMEMADE BREAD

Oblivious to life beyond the latest fashions and the beautiful sweater I'd just purchased, I walked out of the store at the Plaza Shopping Center.

The second I opened the door and stepped onto the sidewalk, the smell hit me. There's nothing more alluring than the aroma of fresh baked bread.

I was being seduced. I hurried down the Plaza sidewalk, enticed. I already felt hungry, and this wonderful smell just compounded it. Finally, the diner door came into view.

I hurried into the restaurant, found a vacant booth, and sat down. My stomach growled.

A young waitress rushed right to my table and graciously took my order for a salad the size of Kentucky. Just as quickly, she returned with two homemade, fresh baked rolls. Aha! I had found the treasure that lured me into the diner.

Warm, fresh bread with melted butter? I took a bite and I

floated, very much like the Hanna Barbara cartoon dog, Snuggles. He floats every time he eats a treat. I was in heaven. I was certain of it.

"These dinner rolls are delicious." I smiled as the waitress set my salad in front of me.

"Oh! Tim made the rolls. He's in the kitchen. Want to tell him yourself?" She smiled back at me.

"Sure. I'd love to meet the genius who baked this bread."

A minute later, as I focused on creating the perfect forkful of fresh vegetables, I heard a voice. "Hi. My name is Tim."

I glanced up and got lost as I looked into the kindest brown eyes I'd ever seen, though the dark circles underneath them didn't escape me. There was a mixture of gentleness and sadness all around this man.

I glanced down at his apron, and stained as it was, it couldn't disguise his emaciated body. He looked like he hadn't slept or eaten in days.

"Hi." I put my fork down. "I'm Barbara. I love your rolls. I just wanted you to know. You're very talented."

"Thank you." Tim pointed to the seat across from me. "Mind?"

"No, not at all." Surprised, I raised my eyebrows, and followed Tim's movements as he sat down.

Sliding into the booth, he folded his hands together on the table, his thumbs nervously fidgeting with one another. He looked across at me and tried to smile.

"I used to do a lot more baking, but not so much anymore. A year or so ago my son committed suicide."

Totally caught off guard, I jerked back in my seat while my eyes nearly popped out of my head. All manners flew out the window. "What happened?" I blurted.

Tim talked for quite a while. One morning he got up and set about his day as usual, only to discover too late that his only son had secretly been very unhappy.

I forgot all about my lunch as I sat and listened to a man whose life had been unexpectedly turned upside down. This was the second time in my young life that a stranger had blindsided me by sharing the insidious, piercing wound of family suicide.

Twenty minutes passed in a flash, and before I knew it, Tim said he needed to return to the kitchen. I promised to come back for lunch again, and we said our goodbyes.

I felt wounded. I felt cold. I sensed there was meant to be more, that somehow there was a deeper reason for our meeting. But I didn't know what that reason was. There hadn't been an opportunity for it to present itself.

Fragments of my time with Tim followed me for days. For quite a while I'd wake up to the image of him sitting across from me at the diner, his gentle eyes searching mine for answers, crying out for a lifeline as giant waves of grief and defeat tried to pull him under.

For days after we met my insides shook, not just because of what was shared, but by the way it had come to be shared.

For the first time ever, I felt sadness like never before. Something unusual was happening in my life, and while I noticed it, I did not understand it.

The thing is, I had no concept of faith at that time. Again, I had no knowledge of Jesus, of His gifts, or of a triune God. I only knew what Hope Danbury had shared with me, which wasn't much.

I wanted to settle down, and enjoy marriage, a family, and career, just like my friends. Instead, life kept throwing me unexpected curve balls: things I simply couldn't explain.

Frankly, it scared me.

Tim was quite a bit older than I was. I did go back to the diner a few times to say hello. But eventually, life led me down a different trail.

CHAPTER 4

I Knew It All Along

You know, time does not stop passing us by just because we might want it to. Before I knew it, I was twenty-one years old.

Well, I had gone and done it. I married the man my mother thought was perfect for me. Keith was an attorney, nine years my senior.

Finally, I was about to live the life I had always wanted.

Sure.

Not only was Keith the wrong man for me, but five years into our marriage, at the young age of thirty-five, he had a stroke. Seemingly out of nowhere, he went blind and fell into a coma for three days. And as if that wasn't enough, while in the coma he was violent, strapped to a hospital bed, yelling my name all the way down the hospital corridor.

I was twenty-six years old. What happened was so frightening to me, so surreal, I went on auto pilot.

My husband was taken to the hospital in the wee hours of the morning, and I believe with all my heart and soul that the nurses on duty were angels in disguise.

Very gently, they guided me to Keith's bedside. They suggested I sit and talk to him. They claimed that even in the coma, he would be able to hear my voice.

So, for three days, sleep deprived, terrified, confused, running on coffee and adrenaline, I sat by Keith's beside and talked to him. And on the third morning, before dawn, he woke up!

He opened his eyes and looked right at me. Then, quietly he said, "Hello."

I shrieked! Before me was a man who had spent most of three days thrashing about, suddenly talking to me calmly, as though nothing had happened.

Scared to death by the unexpected greeting, I jumped out my chair. I'm surprised I didn't give Keith a heart attack as I bolted out of his room.

Did he know me? Was he okay?

I ran to the nurses' desk and shouted at them that my husband was awake!

Well, Keith was perfectly fine. No paralysis. No damage to his eyesight. No speech impairment. Other than abnormally high blood pressure that could be controlled with medication, the man was healed.

I, on the other hand, was a wreck. Thirty-five-year-old men are not supposed to go blind in the middle of the night from high blood pressure.

I did the only thing I knew to do. Once Keith was home and settled, I went shopping.

I was certain that shopping would distract me and ease the fears constantly swarming about inside of me. Maybe a break would help me sleep better at night. Every time I went to bed, I held my breath.

Would Keith be okay if I fell asleep?

So, I went to the nearby mall. I walked into a dress shop, said hello to the woman working behind the counter, and passed out cold from the shock of what had occurred.

Dreams of fire, people in psychological pain, people in comas listening to my voice; yes, God's prophetic call on my life began very early.

Keith recovered from the stroke, and not long after, the two of us went on vacation out of the country to St. Martin. Sun, beach, ocean, good food, it was what most people would call a once in a lifetime trip.

The long plane ride finally ended, and we landed on a tiny airstrip. We got into a taxi, I looked over at my husband, and said to him, "We need to go back home."

Keith turned his head, looked at me, and laughed.

"No, I'm not joking. We need to go home."

"Yeah, right." My husband turned away from me and looked out the car window at the white sand peeking through the trees. It was a beautiful day, and he wasn't about to let anything spoil the trip.

However, I felt upset the whole week we were there, and I couldn't pinpoint the reason.

Keith and I were shown to our cabana. It was right on the beach.

Ours were lazy, sunny afternoons, one right after another, exquisite sunsets and the sound of crystal clear, aqua blue water washing against the shoreline each night. No one in their right mind would want to leave.

But I did.

And when we finally arrived home a week later, we learned that shortly after we had left, Keith's father had suddenly passed away from an unexpected heart attack. No one knew how to reach us. Well, except the Holy Spirit.

Occurrences such as this were becoming more and more common in my life.

Walking with God's gifts of prophecy, revelation, His healing presence, His knowledge, and His mercy, without knowing what they were, or whose they were, was ridiculously difficult, disturbing, and often quite frightening.

As born-again believers, we've been created to flourish in God's gifts, and to delight in them. But first, we have to know about them and learn all we can about them. We need to know all about Jesus.

It was never meant that I be scared of a supernatural life with God. And every time I thought I'd found the answers that made sense of such seemingly odd occurrences, God would orchestrate something else, something incredibly astounding that told me I was way off base. What I thought were answers dropped by the wayside.

He would also make certain I somehow crossed paths with the name of Jesus.

And while with time, I learned to accept the Lord's name and feel comfortable with it, it still never occurred to me He wanted me to make Him my Lord and Savior.

My husband and I eventually parted ways. I am saddened to say his father's death set off a series of events that left us both miles apart, in every kind of way.

I was close to thirty years old. I knew now I was "different" than other people. I just didn't know what to make of it. Facing divorce, I found myself smack dab in the middle of a huge life transition.

CHAPTER 5

THE FISTS OF DARKNESS

Dan Baxter? Oh no! I felt like my head was going to explode.

I listened to the dean's voice on the other end of the phone. The good news was I'd been granted a university graduate assistantship. The bad news was the assistantship was with Dr. Dan Baxter.

I broke into a cold sweat.

Graduate school was uncharted territory. Somehow, I'd been accepted into a master's level Community Counseling program and was finishing my first year. I'd survived, though I don't know how.

The expectations for students in this program were high. I was expected to maintain A's and B's throughout the whole program.

I had been analyzed, videotaped, encouraged, discouraged, and now this? Dan Baxter, head of Group Counseling, had a reputation for being tough. If anyone could pull down a student's grade point average, it was him.

The day came for us to meet. I felt like I was about to face a firing squad.

I can do this, I said to myself as I reluctantly trudged from the elevator to his office. The door was open, so I stood by it and softly knocked.

"Hi!" The tall, bald man greeted me exuberantly. The sound of his loud, deep voice jarred my already raw nerves.

"I'm Dr. Baxter. You must be Barbara! My wife and I had seven children, but now just six." He smiled as he walked over to me and stuck out his hand for me to shake.

What in the world? What an odd way to greet someone. Why would he share with me, a stranger, something as personal as an obvious loss of a child?

Dr. Baxter's right hand was still extended for me to shake. I hesitantly took it with my own, looked into his eyes, and unsuccessfully tried to force a smile onto my face.

Ouch! What was that? It was all I could do to stand still, to not step back, far away from this man.

You see, the second Dr. Baxter took my hand, I immediately felt a harsh blow, fast and forceful to the middle of my stomach. It felt as though someone had punched me!

The professor was still smiling, which told me he must not

40

have felt anything. Just me? What's going on?

I could barely focus during our meeting. No one's ever going to believe this. Something was very wrong. I did my best at pretending to care about what was being said, but truthfully, I just wanted out of there.

Finally, we were done. Totally unnerved, I stood, thanked the professor for his time, and walked out of his office.

I felt doomed. I couldn't help thinking, as I approached the elevator, that my career as a counselor had just ended before my very eyes.

Shortly after that unusual introduction, the second year of grad school began. Over time, I discovered that the rumors about Dr. Baxter weren't true. I liked that he held high standards when it came to teaching.

He truly cared about people. His passion and enthusiasm were contagious, and I always felt encouraged.

Whatever had happened when we first shook hands thankfully never reoccurred. Eventually, I forgot about it and became friends with the whole Baxter family.

His children were grown and scattered, and often I'd spend time at his house and visit with his wife, Sue. Once I even traveled with them out of state to visit their daughter, Anna. I was honored. I was happy.

That is, until life blew up in all our faces.

It was a spectacular fall afternoon. The sun was shining, leaves were turning colors, and the air was crisp, filled with infinite possibilities as we approached the holidays.

I was at the Baxter house, seated at the dining room table. Sue sat across from me making Halloween cutouts for her grandchildren. I watched, and we talked for a while about all kinds of things like kids, recipes, and Thanksgiving.

Eventually, their little dog, Noodles, trotted over to greet me. She sat at my side and waited for me to bend down and scratch a hello behind her ears. Once she felt properly acknowledged, she walked underneath the table, laid down, and rested her chin on my right foot.

As Noodles made herself comfortable, Professor Baxter charged into the room, just long enough to grab his car keys. "See you later," he yelled as he all but flew out the door.

I looked at Sue and grinned, expecting her to do the same. Instead, I watched her lay down her scissors and frown across the table at me.

"What is it?" I saw tears forming in her normally clear, blue eyes.

"He's always rushing. And he's always busy." She picked up the scissors again, along with a piece of orange construction paper. She looked at her hands, shook her head, and slammed everything back down on the table.

The tears were now streaming down her cheeks.

"We had a little boy," she began. "His name was Michael. He was two. One day he was playing outside, when Dan rushed out the door, in a hurry to get to class, just like now." She stopped, looked down at the cluttered table, and tried to find a breath.

I sat as still as possible, feeling suddenly frightened by Sue's behavior.

"Dan got in the car and didn't see Michael behind him. He just didn't see him. He backed up and…and…"

"Oh my God!" I heard myself say those words, though truthfully everything became instantly fuzzy. I wanted to rush over and hug Sue, but the impact of such an unexpected confession tied me to my chair. I could barely move.

It was all I could do to reach across the table for her hand and hold on tight as she wiped her wet cheeks. Shocked and suddenly speechless, my hand never left hers as she talked more about Michael and the rest of her family.

Dr. Baxter had accidently backed his car over his two-year-old son and killed him.

To this day, I still don't know what to say.

Barbara Beck

CHAPTER 6

The Thief Does Kill

Eventually, there would come a time when I could process what I experienced that fall day. The things I heard helped to explain the "punch" to my stomach when I touched Dr. Baxter's hand, and his odd statement when we'd just met about having seven children, though now only six.

But on that particular day, as I sat with Sue, nothing seemed real. I waited and waited, certain someone would walk into the room and tell us it was all a cruel joke.

Except, no one did.

You know, it's one thing to be with a person when they share with me the sadness and pain that loss can bring. It's quite another to sit and share in the type of agony that can rip a soul to shreds. As I sat with Sue, I felt a kind of terror and horror I'd never known; the terror that says that at any minute life can shatter a person's heart and shred it into pieces.

No one should ever have to experience that.

My thoughts were all over the place when I drove home that day.

For the first time ever, I felt the powerful force of grief and darkness that Dr. Baxter carried inside of him. I had felt it as a real, physical blow to my stomach the first day I met him and shook his hand.

This was something new to me. It was not another mere scenario of two people whose hearts and/or bodies might have needed healing. This was beyond what I was learning in my counseling classes, and certainly bigger than my present prayers. I didn't understand what was happening.

All I knew was that there was a powerful, physical force behind pain and darkness that wanted its deadly way.

Adrenaline shot through my body as I allowed my heart to glimpse the magnitude of what was occurring.

Suddenly panicked, my hands glued themselves tightly to the steering wheel. Every muscle in my body stiffened as question after question raced through my mind.

How would I describe this to my friends? How could I even try, without breaking a personal and professional confidence?

"What do I do with it all, God?" I asked out loud. My swollen eyes hurt from crying, and I desperately needed a Kleenex.

I thought I'd never get home.

Finally, I pulled into my driveway. I sat for a moment in my car. I took a deep breath, then pulled the keys out of the ignition.

Though I felt exhausted, thoughts kept racing through my head. I had no idea why I had been made privy to such horrific family tragedy, or why I was able to feel the physical force of darkness. However, I did know this: I was somehow meant to be a light in the Baxter family.

I don't know how I knew it. I just did, the same way I had no doubt there was more to come. I could not tell you details. I had no idea of "how, what, when, where, or why." I only knew there was more.

I felt very unsettled, to say the least.

I knew that one day all my questions would have answers. But for now, I could only hope that by being a friend, maybe, just maybe, it would help the family heal. I prayed it would.

I left the car, walked to my front door, and went inside. My heart bruised and battered, I reached the kitchen counter and set down my purse and car keys. Dragging myself to the bedroom, I fell onto the bed.

My last thoughts before falling asleep were about the future. Perhaps now the professor and his family could truly begin to move forward. Maybe Sue had taken a first step by talking about what had happened, and the eye of the storm had passed.

Right?

The call came a few weeks later.

I was awake, sitting at my usual spot in the living/dining area of the townhouse. The sun wasn't up yet, and I treasured the quiet of early morning. I was writing another paper for school, and desperately needed to focus.

I'm comfortable in the calm of early morning, which is why the shrill of the phone about gave me a heart attack.

"Barb, it's Kate! Barb, it's awful!" My classmate and closest friend at school, Kate Robbins, was sobbing on the other end of the phone line.

I couldn't imagine what had happened. So, I waited quietly until her tears seemed to subside.

"What?" I asked.

"An avalanche!"

"A what? Kate, what are you talking about?"

"Barb, I'm so sorry. I know you are close. I'm so sorry. Barb, there was an avalanche. Dr. Baxter's son, James, was skiing with friends in Colorado. There was…um…no one survived, Barb!"

"How do you know?" My hands began to shake. I couldn't quite grasp what Kate was saying. I stood up, and so did the hair on my arms.

"Dean Jensen called me right before I called you. He probably thought it best if you heard the news first from a friend. There was a group of four boys. No survivors. I guess Dr. Baxter and

Sue are on their way to Colorado right now."

I couldn't think. I sat back down. I listened. But I couldn't think.

"Kate…um… thanks for calling me." I was just about to explain to her that I needed some time to absorb the news, when I heard call waiting click on the phone line.

"Um, Kate, there's another call coming through. I'm going to take it, and I'll call you later. Okay?"

CHAPTER 7

Going Through the Motions

"Hello." My voice was flat.

"Barbara?" The soft voice I heard was tentative.

"Anna? Oh Anna, I can't believe this!" I started to cry. Then Anna, the Baxters' daughter, began to cry. For a moment we just let our tears say more than words ever could.

"Barb, my parents are on their way to Colorado. There's an investigation, a search for bodies, and a bunch of reporters. It's a nightmare. In the meantime, while they're headed to Colorado, there's another reporter that wants to come to Michigan for an interview, to my parents' house near you and the university.

"That reporter should be there tomorrow at 1:00 p.m. Barb, can you come? I'm catching a flight there tonight. Please, could you come over and be with me when the reporter comes?"

"Of course, Anna. What else can I do? What about Noodles?"

"The neighbors will care for her until I get there. Barb, pray.

Please pray hard. I'll see you tomorrow."

Anna thanked me between more tears. The sound of her shaky voice tore at my already shattered heart.

I stood and gazed vacantly around the room. For a moment, I didn't recognize where I was or what to do. I just stood.

Then, I felt a rush of heat inside of me, the kind of heat that rises and swells and intensifies. Suddenly I was consumed with rage, like never before.

"Dear God," I cried out. "What are you doing? Why? Why the Baxter family, God? Haven't they suffered enough? Every time I turn around, someone tells me of horrendous loss in that family. And now this? I don't understand you!"

I fell to my knees and sobbed. I was so angry all I could do was cry.

I stayed there quite a while, until there were no more tears. Then, in a fog, I sat back on my haunches, and tried once again to grasp the unbelievable news I'd just received.

I did eventually pray for the Baxter family. Even though I wasn't yet saved and didn't yet know Jesus, my life was so intensely odd most of the time, that I often turned to God.

I knew nothing about warfare, armor, protection, or His love. I simply believed God could hear me. So, I prayed to Him, out loud. Well, first I yelled at Him, still outraged.

Then through watery eyes, with soaked cheeks and a broken heart, I asked God to help Dr. Baxter, Sue, and the rest of their family.

A few weeks passed, then school was out for Thanksgiving break. It had been all I could do to finish my fall classes.

Dr. Baxter turned in his resignation. Spring would be his last semester at the university. Following graduation, he and his wife planned to move to White Plains, NY to be with Anna.

My insides were crushed. My heart hurt like no other time in my life. I had no clue what the future would bring, and I did not care.

The people closest to me, those I had spent most of my time with for almost two years, people I loved, were not only leaving, but going with torn, ripped hearts. And there was nothing I could do about it.

I had hoped graduate school would be one of the greatest experiences of my life. Instead, it had turned out to be one of the most frightening, unusual, painful two years I had ever known.

I felt all alone, constantly chased by grief and fear from what had happened.

Someone recently asked me if I stayed in touch with Professor Baxter and his family.

Well, purely by God's grace, we all finished the school year. I completed the assistantship and graduated. The Baxters' house sold at the end of the summer, and they left town.

I stayed in contact with Sue for a while. However, over time life seemed to take us in different directions. I tell myself that, though I suppose they were doing their best to heal and move on. I was a reminder of one of the worst experiences in their already battered lives.

My relationship with Dr. Baxter, himself, had never been anything except professional. Because he was my mentor and professor, there was an unspoken rule between us that did not allow us to talk about our deep, personal lives.

I did not bring up what Sue had confided to me about Michael. If she, herself, had told her husband what she had shared, he never let on to me.

Dr. Baxter remained rooted in his professional, vivacious cover up of pain. Looking back, I can only guess that he desperately needed an exuberant persona. I believe he walked a tightrope of denial, without a net.

However, none of his ways or all that happened kept me from caring about this man and his family. As you might imagine, I had quite an assortment of thoughts and feelings to sort through.

I respected the professional boundaries Dr. Baxter upheld. I did my best to be a friend to Sue and Anna. I obviously was made privy to darkness, and for some reason, was asked to pray and be a light. That much I understood.

During my time with the Baxter family, I tried to talk about what happened with a few close friends. But no one was able to help me understand. They did not know Jesus.

None of us did.

CHAPTER 8

WHOSE SIDE ARE YOU ON?

To say I was a different person after graduate school would be an understatement.

It took quite a while for me to come to terms with what had basically been two years of heartache and confusion.

How did I heal from all of it?

I didn't. I ran.

I pursued a doctorate degree and began right after I received a master's degree.

I chose a school out of state, threw myself into classes, and tried to adjust to a totally new, highly competitive environment.

Of course, it didn't work. Exhausted and burned out, I returned home after a year.

Once I felt rested, I decided to take a road trip from Ohio, where I lived, to Washington D.C. My heart needed a chance to mend from the horror of recent years. I wanted to get away and visit my aunt and uncle.

Driving on the Pennsylvania turnpike, singing loudly off key with pop tunes on the radio, I looked down and noticed I was low on gas. Hmm, better stop.

Now, this was back in the day when there were service stations. Someone, usually a man, would come to your car window, ask what you want, and in addition to pumping gas for you, would not only wash your windshield, but check your oil as well.

Those were the days.

I pulled off the turnpike into a large service station and parked next to a pump. I opened the door and got out, needing a good stretch.

"Hi." A tall, white-haired gentleman dressed in navy work pants and a navy jacket, walked up to the car. "What'll it be?"

"Fill it, please." I threw my arms over my head and began twisting right, then left.

After starting the gas pump, the older gentlemen opened the hood of the car. As he reached for the dip stick to check the oil, I heard him clearly say to me, "I've been waiting for you."

"Uh, I beg your pardon?" I lowered my arms. This man now had my full attention.

"I've been waiting for you. I knew you were coming." He stopped what he was doing, turned, and looked at me.

"My wife died of cancer a few years ago. Then my son got sick and passed away a few months ago. It comes in threes, you know."

Totally shocked, all I could think to say was, "I will pray for you."

"Please do. My name is John. Your car is fine. You will have a safe, comfortable journey."

"Thank you." I looked into John's gentle brown eyes.

He nodded, then turned and washed my windshield. When he was done, he collected my money and said goodbye.

I stood next to the gas pump, and watched John slowly walk away. I gave my head a quick shake, stunned by what had just happened.

After a few seconds, I found my voice. I spoke out loud as I asked God to please protect John's heart from further loss, pain, and heartache.

So, right about now dear readers, there's a good chance you might be thinking, this author is nuts.

Well, that's just my point.

There were so many unusual encounters in my life that occurred before I was saved, that I often questioned my sanity.

This trip was one of those times.

I did not grow up with permission to know God, or His anointing, or His angels, or His Son. I was barely taught to believe God was, well, just God. Thus, I had no clue what was happening in my life.

It never occurred to me to ask anyone either, especially a pastor, about what was going on. Why would I?

I didn't know anything about the power of prayer, or spiritual warfare, or miracles.

Instead, I simply learned to accept the "odd" encounters, to pray if asked, and mostly keep quiet.

As time went on, I repeatedly tried to bury the fear and loneliness I felt in my heart.

Of course, it didn't work.

Looking back, I can see now that starting at an early age, God placed a very powerful, prophetic call on my life.

And I believe beyond all doubt that He faithfully kept me safe, kept me from getting in the way of His gifts for me, and kept the call on my life protected.

That is, until such a time as this.

PART TWO

FANNING THE FLAMES

CHAPTER 9

When in Doubt, Retreat

Being back home in Ohio helped me to relax a bit, but ultimately did nothing to explain the unusual events in my life. I felt lost and out of sorts no matter where I went or what I did.

Concerned as well as discouraged, I made plans to take a vacation. I decided to visit a colleague, a fellow counselor, and attend her weeklong retreat in Montana.

My goal? To figure out once and for all what I truly wanted from life. It was the 1980s. Women were supposed to be able to "have it all," whatever that meant. I just assumed it was my job to figure that all out.

Never in my wildest imagination would I have guessed that it wasn't about figuring out what I might want in life. It was about discovering a whole new truth, and what our triune God might want for my life.

The moment I stepped off the small prop plane, I fell in love with Montana. I was surrounded by huge, majestic, stunning mountains. Just looking at them, I felt better than I had in quite a while.

Long morning hikes in cool, crispy air acted like a healing balm to my weary soul. I slept like a log each night, and for the first time in a very long time, I woke each morning with anticipation.

Though I felt hopeful in general and enjoyed my colleagues, I confess I had placed a lot of expectation on this retreat. As the days flew by, I realized I wanted to have a life altering experience. I was sure I would leave with a definite new plan and direction for my future.

Well, the next day would be my last day at the retreat. And so far, nothing had happened. The idea of returning back to Ohio the same as when I came was disturbing.

"Okay everyone. Can I have your attention for a moment?" My colleague's voice rang out clear as a bell above the buzz of the group.

Suzanne was short, though physically fit. Her chin-length blond hair swayed back and forth as she easily climbed onto the seat of a wooden chair.

"As you know," she began, "tomorrow is our last day together.

So tonight, I'm giving you homework." She smiled as the room filled with moans and groans.

"I want everyone to take home a sheet of white poster board, and a box of colored pencils. Those things are on the table by the door.

"Tonight, I want you to draw a circle in the middle of the posterboard. Make it as large as you can, and color it in any way you want."

The room buzzed again with comments and laughter.

"People, I don't want you to think. Just color. See where it takes you. There's no right or wrong to this. Just let what's inside of you come out tonight. Have fun!"

Fun? Really?

As I watched Suzanne jump down from her chair, a vision came to me, much more appealing than our homework assignment. I saw myself in comfy sweats, a loaded pizza beside me, and a movie playing on the television.

I sighed, as instead I picked up a sheet of poster board, a box of pencils, and headed out the door, back to the B & B where I was staying.

Of course, I had no idea what to do. I sat on the floor in my room, crossed my legs, stuck my right elbow on my knee, and rested my head on the fist of my right hand.

Hmm. I stared at the posterboard while frustration grew into out and out resentment. I was odd. My life was odd. Maybe I should just draw the pizza.

It took another half hour or so for me to work through the feelings of self-pity. Finally, I realized that lamenting wasn't going to help. So, I picked up a pencil. It was orange.

I began to color inside the huge circle I had drawn, and once I started, I began to enjoy myself. It was as if the pencil had taken on a life of its own, and I didn't want to stop. Go figure.

After a while, I put down the orange pencil and picked up a red one. Before I was done, I'd added a touch of blue, and just a hint of yellow. When I looked at the clock, I was surprised to find that more than a couple of hours had passed.

With a yawn, I put away the colored pencils. I had no idea why I did what I did, and truthfully didn't care. I was tired.

I got up from the floor, brushed my teeth, pulled back the covers, and practically fell into bed.

And it seemed as though I had just fallen asleep when daylight snuck into the room and nudged me from a sound sleep.

Morning already? Coffee?

Opening my eyes, I stretched for a moment before I climbed out of bed.

As I did, I couldn't help but reflect. I didn't believe the retreat had necessarily helped me.

Oh well, at least I'd had the courage to come. And I suppose it was relaxing.

I dressed. I combed my hair. I rolled up my posterboard, put a rubber band around it, grabbed my shoulder bag, and left for the nearest Starbucks.

A retreat is not a retreat without morning coffee

CHAPTER 10

AGAIN? REALLY?

I walked into the noisy room. Conversations buzzed everywhere.

Either everyone in the group had also stopped at Starbucks for a caffeine fix, or they were anxious to share their homework with one another. Perhaps there was some of both contributing to this morning's decibel level.

The chairs were set up today in a semi-circle, facing Suzanne. It looked as though she was planning to call upon each one of us individually, to come up in front of the group and share our drawings.

As I stood, it quickly dawned on me that Suzanne probably expected to hear from each of us about some great, life-changing thought that occurred as we each drew on our posterboard last night.

I was doomed. I didn't have any new realizations to share.

I was about to be irrevocably embarrassed this morning. I just knew it.

I turned toward the door and prepared to slink out of the room before everyone took their seats.

"Oh! Hi Barb!" One of the group members saw me, stuck her arm up, and waved enthusiastically.

I had no choice but to wave back, while the rest of the group lifted their heads.

Busted.

Oh no. It was my turn.

I stood up and unrolled my poster board.

Suzanne gasped. "Oh my gosh!"

She startled me. I looked from her to my posterboard, then back at her.

"What? Is it that awful?" My worst fears were coming true.

"Oh my gosh! Barbara! That's fire! You drew a circle of fire!"

I looked at the poster again and sure enough, there was a huge circle of flames looking back at me. I began to shake, as all the color drained from my face.

Suddenly, Suzanne and the group disappeared. The memory of the dream I'd had at age three flooded my mind, and I was back there. All over again, I stood on the sidewalk and watched the huge flames across the street dance up to the sky.

"Are you okay?" Suzanne's voice sounded far, far away, as

though she was calling me from the other end of a long tunnel.

She guided me to a nearby chair. "You're white as a sheet. Sit down."

With a blank face, I turned to Suzanne. I couldn't think of anything to say, so I just stood there.

I stared at the posterboard while Suzanne settled me into the chair.

I had never mentioned the dream of fire to anyone. It's not that I'd forgotten about it. I just rarely, if ever, shared any of the events in my life.

And here it was, fire, once again staring me in the face, this time in front of a group of people.

I felt my bones succumb to weariness, my shoulders slump, and resignation permeate my heart.

How was I going to explain this to Suzanne? Was I even supposed to explain this? What should I say?

I came to the retreat feeling "displaced" in life, for lack of better word. Now, today, I was leaving full of fear and confusion. Again.

Suzanne tried to encourage me, excited about the passion she saw on the poster board. She made comments to the group and gave her interpretation of what the drawing meant.

But I didn't hear what she said. The terror of my own life, of the many unexplainable events and circumstances, left me feeling bound and gagged in my chair.

Suzanne moved on to someone else, and the fog in my head

eventually cleared. Like all the other times, I supposed I would just have to pick up in life where I left off before the "odd" occurrence.

I told myself I would go home, go back to work, and forget all about the poster. The thing is, I wasn't sure it would work this time.

Back in Ohio, each day felt like a bigger challenge than the day before. Discouragement turned into deep depression, and I couldn't seem to shake it.

"God, I don't understand." It was a Saturday morning, and having had another restless night, I was sitting on the side of my bed. Tissues that had once filled the purple flowered box on my lap, were now wadded up all over the floor.

Crying hard, I slid off of the side off the mattress. I wrapped my arms around myself, propped my back against the side of the bed, and stared at the wall.

"What is it you're asking from me? Why fire, God? Have I done something wrong?" I could barely whisper the words in between hiccups.

And at that precise second, my eyes swollen and burning, my cheeks soaked, I felt the back of a finger glide softly down the side of my face!

What?

I sat up faster than you could blink! I ran a few fingers down my cheek, certain I would find something there. Dust? A fly?

Okay, there's nothing on my cheek. What just happened?

Suddenly, I felt the top of my hair flutter, as if someone was playing with my curls.

My hand flew to my head.

"Who's there?" Eyes bulging, I spoke out loud to no one, at least no one you could see. I reached for my phone on the nearby bedside table, ready to call 911 and tell them, um…. well…. what exactly could I tell them that wouldn't land me in a psych unit?

Was that You, God? Really? An angel, maybe?

I still did not know Jesus or anything about the Kingdom. I was clearly astounded by what I had just felt.

But interestingly enough, this time something inside was ready to believe. Astonishment turned into excitement. I guess I had had enough experiences to accept that God's ways are indeed supernatural. So maybe…just maybe…He was letting me know that He was listening to me. Maybe it was Him saying, "Yes. I truly do care."

CHAPTER 11

THE POWER OF KINDNESS

Isn't it amazing how much a touch of loving-kindness can impact our lives, especially when it comes as a miracle from God, Himself?

A supernatural act of kindness is the most powerful experience on earth.

I sat still for a long time on my bedroom floor that Saturday.

After quietly trying to absorb what had just happened, I knew only two things: God had been listening to me, and my hiccups were gone.

I was not alone. It was true what my Christian friends had said. If you believe, you're never alone.

They were right about another thing, too. I was important to God. Me, a mere pin prick in all His creation; He wiped away my tears. No one had ever wiped away my tears.

I tried to digest it all, took a breath, and relaxed back against the bed.

As I sat on my bedroom carpet in the middle of a mass of crumpled tissues, looking at a wall no less, I felt a quiet confidence like never before.

"Huh, so this is what peace feels like." I tried to smile.

I reached for a clean tissue, was about to blow my nose, when I realized something else. I felt wide awake, and clear-headed. Stuffy nose and all, for the first time ever, I felt alive enough to know in my heart that I'd been deemed worthy that morning; worthy enough to receive a touch from God.

A few weeks later, I found myself still in awe of that amazing Saturday morning. I wanted more. I was hungrier than ever for another touch from up above.

Finally, I couldn't stand it any longer. I was so stunned by the experience of God's compassion for me that as I passed by a local church one afternoon, I stopped.

I walked into an empty sanctuary, sat down, and closed my eyes.

I have no idea why I chose to stop at a church that day, as opposed to a Jewish temple. I had heard Jesus' name mentioned often, and I was no longer uncomfortable with that. I just still had not considered making Him my Savior.

All I know is that I was still struck by all that had recently happened. I was drawn to the church.

So, I allowed myself to sit and quietly reflect.

Threads of a lifetime of experiences went through my mind; experiences that couldn't be explained in any kind of practical way. I could see now that the events in my life had nothing to do with coincidence, and everything to do with prayer and miracles. For the first time ever, I reflected upon how good God has been in my life, instead of letting fear dominate my thoughts,

As I sat, a vision of Jesus came into my mind. From the shoulders up He was facing me with His right arm stretched toward me. He was silently asking me to take His hand.

The vision startled me. And yet it didn't. Yes, I was surprised because I didn't normally give Jesus much thought. And I had never seen Him before when I closed my eyes.

But deep inside I knew. In fact, I believe I had always somehow known that making Jesus my Lord and Savior was important.

So, with eyes still closed, I reached out my hand to Him and I saw Him take hold of it with His own.

And dear readers, He has yet to let go.

I went home that day and prayed.

After a few days, I returned to the church to talk with the senior pastor. We had a very brief conversation, and I asked Jesus Christ to come into all of me and be my Lord and Savior.

It was a quiet day. It was easy, yet it was one of the most difficult things I've ever done.

The pull inside me to the Lord was so strong, I had somehow found the courage to step out in faith against my entire family.

I felt joy. I felt deep sorrow. I looked forward to church and new friends, and I never felt more alone in my whole life.

A few months later I was baptized in water. Of course, I was nervous and very self-conscious. Looking back, I recall the church was filled with people. A hundred? Possibly. Truthfully, it seemed like the whole world watched.

However, an even a bigger event for me, was the day I received the baptism of the Holy Spirit. That happened unexpectedly while visiting another church with a friend.

I answered an altar call. I had no idea how the baptism of the Holy Spirit would change my life. I simply stood, while the pastor walked by and touched our foreheads.

Some people fell backwards. But I did not. I just felt full of joy, and excited.

Learning who the Holy Spirit is and Who it is I walk with brought me peace like never before. For the first time ever, I felt the fear in me subside. I began to understand myself. That, in and of itself, is a miracle.

Though I knew I had a lot to learn, realizing that our God is a triune God, is Spirit, and is Love, changed my life forever.

Did you know a miracle is like a pebble in the huge pond of creation?

The Lord's act of kindness toward me that Saturday morning long ago caused ripples; endless, eternal, forever flowing ripples, not just in my life, but in the lives of people I'd yet to know.

My life had changed. I felt excited each morning when I woke up. Instead of wanting to hide from things like posterboard and circles of fire, I embraced what I had drawn. It was a symbol to me, of God, of the power of His passionate love inside me.

CHAPTER 12

KNOWLEDGE IS POWER

Not long after becoming a believer, I moved to Arizona. I experienced more sunshine the first three months I was there than I had ever experienced in my entire life.

A short time later, I began attending church. Consistently I sat and listened to Pastor Sam twice a week for close to two years.

Then life exploded. Once again.

I was on the phone one evening with my friend, Peg, from Ohio. I listened as she spoke to me about something called spiritual gifts.

"Spiritual gifts? What is that?" I abandoned all my manners, stuffed a big potato chip into my mouth, and crunched in Peg's ear.

"You never heard of spiritual gifts? Where have you been?"

That's what I loved most about Peg. She didn't put on any airs about anything.

"Peg," I said, taking a quick swig of Dr. Pepper, "I did not grow up in the church, like you. Remember?"

"Yeah, but still, after two years at the church I just assumed one of your pastors would have talked about them. What kind of church are you going to?"

"I don't know. A Christian one. Why?"

Peg laughed. "You, of all people, need to know about the gifts."

And with that, she proceeded to tell me.

I listened.

Then I listened more.

I even put my Dr. Pepper down on the counter and forgot all about the bag of chips.

I was enthralled. I was upset. I don't know what I was.

Peg was thorough. She asked me to open my Bible and follow along as she read from the book of Corinthians

"But the manifestation of the Spirit is given to each one for mutual profit: for to one is given the word of wisdom by the Spirit, to another the word of knowledge by the same Spirit, to another Faith by the same Spirit, to another gifts of healing by the same Spirit, to another working of miracles, to another prophecy, to another discerning of spirits, to another different kinds of tongues, to another the interpretation of tongues. But one and the same Spirit works all these things, dividing to each one individually as He wills."
(1 Cor. 12:7-11 NKJV).

Next, she read from the book of Romans, explaining things as she went along.

"Having then gifts differing according to the grace that is given to us, let us use them: if prophecy, let us prophesy in proportion to our faith; or ministry, let us use it in our ministering; he who teaches, in teaching; or he who exhorts, in exhortation; he who gives, with liberality; he who leads, with diligence; he who shows mercy, with cheerfulness"
(Romans 12:6-8).

When she finished, neither of us spoke for what seemed like an eternity. I sat, as anger rose inside of me like a volcano about to erupt.

Finally, I broke the silence, my voice escalating with every word.

"You mean to tell me that for practically my whole life, since I was three, three years old, God's been showing me the gifts He wants me to have, and I didn't even know it? How come no one ever told me about this?"

Poor Peg. I was livid, and she bore the brunt.

After I calmed down and we hung up, it took a while for me to get a handle on the feelings inside me. In fact, for weeks after that conversation, I felt every bit as angry as I did when I first heard Peg explain things to me. I felt betrayed and cheated.

So, I sought books. I read. I studied. And I learned I was not crazy at all. Almighty God, Himself, had gifted me.

My relationship with Him began to rapidly change. I

embraced the way He created me, and paid attention to little else. I became totally absorbed in what I was learning and felt so excited, I failed to notice there was tension at church, mounting in the congregation.

One evening I walked into the sanctuary, and instantly felt as though someone had tied a ball and chain around my ankle. The air was thick and too heavy to ignore. I looked around and saw that the Sunday smiles which had greeted me for two years, had turned upside down into frowns.

The pastor came to the pulpit, and almost immediately he announced he was leaving. After that day, everyone scattered.

It was a split. Half the congregation left the church, leaving behind a wake of feelings of abandonment, broken relationships, grief, and confusion.

Thankfully I had no idea why it happened. I was spared the pain of division. All I knew was life had changed. Again.

CHAPTER 13

THE GREEN-EYED MONSTER

It did not take long for me to find another church to attend. A friend of mine invited me to a wedding, and when I heard the pastor perform the ceremony, I was certain he was to be my new leader.

Jesus was different at my new church than how He had been at my former one. At the new church, we invited the Holy Spirit to join us at each service.

For the first time ever, I began to feel comfortable with God's presence in my life. I met others who shared my beliefs and were open to the way of life I knew.

Shortly after I arrived at the new church, the Lord began to use me. God was, is, and always will be in the miracles business. Praise Jesus!

So, at most services, I'd walk into the sanctuary, stand for praise, and start to worship. Not long after we began to sing, the

Holy Spirit would show me who, around me, needed the Lord's healing presence.

Discreetly, I would point to those people.

After a short time, the pastor began to realize what was happening, and trust me. If someone I pointed to did not go to altar call for the manifestation of God's healing presence, the pastor would contact him during the following week.

People also experienced miracles of healing in my private therapy practice. Moms came to the Lord. Prison inmates called me for prayer and reconciled with their families after years of heartbreak. All glory to God.

With time, I became a testimony to the words of Isaiah:

> *"It shall come to pass That before they call, I will answer; And while they are still speaking, I will hear (Isaiah 64:24).*

Church was exciting for those of us who believed.

Unfortunately, though, it didn't last.

As you know by now, I did not grow up going to church. So, it never dawned on me that anyone there, including leadership, would flat out lie to me while wearing a smile.

As a believer, I strongly support true fellowship. We are meant to come together and bring along Jesus' presence, to gather and share with one another the same intimacy and transparency that we experience during our time with the Lord at home.

There is great power when people come together in Spirit and in truth, in our Lord's name. And our enemy will use whoever he can try and stop it.

Betrayal by Christians, especially church leaders, hurts. There are mean Christians. Dear readers, we are in a spiritual battle, and there are dangerous Christian people prone to slander, gossip, and lies. There are those who intentionally want to stop true ministry and leadership in its tracks.

Of course, there are wonderful, honest Christian people, also. It's just that at my new, small church, I was unexpectedly introduced to the opposite, to the trials, tribulation, and persecution Jesus talks about in the book of Matthew.

Ouch. Unfortunately, this just perpetuated the fear and anxiety I already carried inside.

However, Jesus also, in the book of Matthew, gave us a way out of nasty scenarios. And though early in my walk the Holy Spirit guided me to His words, I did not necessarily like what He had to say.

"You have heard that it was said, 'You shall love your neighbor and hate your enemy.' But I say to you, love your enemies, bless those who curse you, do good to those who hate you, and pray for those who spitefully use you and persecute you," (Matthew 5:43,44).

Love my enemies?

Seriously?

So, much to my dismay at the time, I learned how to pray for my enemies very specifically, according to the situation at hand. I learned to "go to my brother," one on one, and confront difficult issues. I learned how to do good to others who clearly hated me, and to bless people who cursed me.

Most importantly, I learned to submit to our triune God, to forgive simply because Jesus says to forgive. And while this process was not necessarily fun, it has turned out to be one of the most valuable lessons I have ever learned.

Someone asked me recently what exactly happened at the little church I've talked about. And frankly, I can barely remember.

As a result of obeying the Word in Matthew, I am cocooned in the power of the name of our Lord, Jesus. I have remained innocent, as well as protected by God's heavenly hosts of angels.

I intend to keep it this way forever.

By following God's Word, by speaking forgiveness regardless of how I have felt about betrayal by Christians, the Lord has been able to restore just about every single relationship the enemy ever once tried to steal.

What a wonderful statement to be able to make. Over the course of years, He has set a table before my enemies, and He's still adding placemats.

Well, eventually I shook the dust from the small church I had been attending. Of all things, I became an e-member at a church that's located in Kansas City, Missouri.

I was a pioneer in virtual church.

I loved it. For five years I listened, prayed, and studied with members of an online ministry. I grew and grew in knowledge and revelation. I became comfortable with myself, and the various ways the Lord's prophecies wove in and out of my daily life.

PART THREE

A LOOK AT THE OTHER SIDE

CHAPTER 14

DREAMS, DREAMS, AND FLYING MACHINES

My dear readers, I'd like to take a minute now and reflect.

You might already know this, but following Jesus is often like being in the middle of the ocean with only a surfboard.

Just when I thought I had things all figured out, well... what can I say?

After attending the online church, I truly thought I had a handle on what my life should look like. I felt more content than ever. I would work, be part of a great church, and enjoy new friends. Someday I would retire, maybe travel, and eat all the chocolate cake I want.

Right?

"Joan, what do you think? Should I move?"

I was sitting on an empty bleacher facing an empty ball field. Nearby was a park full of barking dogs, laughing kids, and worn-out parents.

The afternoon sun tried to coax the bite out of an April breeze.

I waited impatiently for my best friend to tell me what to do. I felt ready for a change in my life, which both excited me and terrified me. Mostly terrified.

I really liked the online church I had joined. Even from across the country, I felt welcomed and a part of the congregation.

But it wasn't the same as being there in person.

I was ready once again to meet new people and was seriously thinking about moving to Kansas City.

"Barb, I can't tell you what to do. Why don't you first visit the church in Kansas City and see how you like it? I'm sure being there in person is a lot different than what you see online."

Hmm. Little did either of us know that Joan's suggestion was actually a prophecy.

I must have exhausted myself thinking about Missouri, because it didn't take long for me to fall asleep that night.

I climbed into bed, reached up, and turned out the lamp on the small table next to me. There was certainly nothing unusual about that.

However, beginning that night, I had three prophetic dreams. Spread over a week, each one turned my world upside down, more real to me than daily life.

Somehow, we just know when a dream is not simply a dream.

In the first, I was with my estranged sister and stepbrother in an airport. My sister kept riding an escalator up and down.

I watched, then went to a table and sat down with my stepbrother. I looked at him and said, "This is the hardest thing you'll ever have to do."

In the second dream, a few nights later, I was on a bleacher, looking out at a green, empty ball field. The field was just like the one by the park I had recently visited.

A man, I believe an angel, sat next to me wearing a ball cap and baseball uniform. He looked out at the diamond and told me the playing field had changed. Then, out of the clouds, came six more heavenly hosts, all dressed in ball caps and uniforms. They were going to help me with what was to come.

In the third dream, two nights after that, an African American man handed me all his keys, and asked me to go with him on a journey. I said yes.

The following week, the first week of May, I received a phone call from my sister. It was the first communication after five years of silence between us.

She conveyed that our father, age ninety-three, was in the

hospital. He had a stomach infection. His much younger wife had come to visit him, gone home, and unexpectedly had a heart attack. She passed away during the night.

My sister explained she was on her way to the hospital in Blue Springs, Missouri. My stepbrother and his wife were already there.

My dad had dementia. I did not know exactly what a "stomach infection" meant, but the whole situation did not sound good.

That evening, I prayed and talked with the Lord, and He prepared me. He told me my father was about to pass away also, and He asked me to go to my father and pray.

So, two days later I was in an airport with my estranged sister and my stepbrother. Hence, dream number one had come to pass.

Next, I found myself sitting in a hospital room with my dad who only sometimes recognized me. My sister, my stepbrother, and his wife were with me. Dad appeared to be fine, sitting up, laughing, eating. According to the doctor, his diagnosis had not changed. He had a stomach infection.

However, I listened to Spirit. To my knowledge, my father had never been to a church, nor to temple services when we were young. He had not given much thought to God at all, at least not that I knew about. If he were to pass away, well, it would not be good.

So, I waited until the others in my family went to dinner while my dad slept. Then I went to the hospital Chaplain's office. To my surprise, even though it was dinner time, he was still there.

I explained to the Chaplain that my father was ill, he had dementia, and he did not know the Lord. Together we returned to my father's room, and we took turns praying. Through my tears, I asked God if He would allow me to somehow know if my father had met Jesus before his life on earth was over.

The next afternoon, Dad rallied for a brief time. With all of us by his bedside, he looked each one of us in the eye with recognition, and clear as a bell, he shared his thoughts and advice about each of our lives.

He told us all sins were forgiven. He said we were washed clean. He told us to celebrate, and not worry. He looked at me and told me my words were important because they were two thousand years old.

My dad was speaking the Gospel. He also gave a prophecy. At that time, I had no thoughts of becoming a minister or writing a book about my life.

It occurred to me that Dad was saying goodbye. And as shocked and excited as I was at his words, so astounded and thankful that the Lord had answered my prayers, I could not help but also feel pain and sadness, fearing what was to come.

There was an atmosphere of stunning tenderness in my father's hospital room that afternoon. The Holy Spirit gripped everyone's heart, as bittersweet tears flowed down all of our cheeks.

None of us knew one another very well. Yet at my dad's words, all the barriers between us vanished as we sat together in indescribable, perfect love.

There was still no indication from the doctors that Dad was ill beyond a stomach infection. As day turned to evening, we stopped at the cafeteria and talked about aftercare for him. We made plans to visit a nursing facility the next day.

However, the following morning, Dad's body unexpectedly began to shut down. The doctors moved him to the ICU.

And one day later, he was gone.

CHAPTER 15

Endings and Beginnings

As I write this, dear readers, I am astounded all over again at the goodness of God. I believe that when the Holy Spirit came to me in three dreams, when He told me my father would pass, when the Lord honored and answered my prayers, that's when I truly began to understand my life in Him, and Him in me.

Because of Jesus, I was able to come to know a God who is a prophetic God, who answers us before we even call out to Him. I was able to pray for my father's salvation as well as witness it, before he went on to heaven.

But that's not all.

You see, the hospital where my father met the Lord was only twenty minutes from my online church, the very one I had been hoping to visit in person.

And after five years of pride and silence, my sister and I visited that church, together!

Dad's passing was clearly a time full of wonders and miracles, as well as sadness.

For the first time ever, I didn't feel afraid. Yes, I cried as my father left us. However, I was also able to rejoice in the blessing of God's prophetic favor over my life, and the mercy He showed my family.

Friends, please know: if you believe, you are not alone. Ever. There is nothing to fear in life. Ever. You are not crazy.

You've been gifted by Almighty God.

The plane ride home dragged on and on. Though I had plenty to think about, I was tired. My eyelids kept drooping.

For a moment I forgot where I was and tried to stretch my legs out in front of me. Needless to say, that didn't work.

I let my eyes close and my thoughts roam. I never knew God cares so deeply about all of us. I was still surprised that He had heard my prayers and answered them in the miraculous way He had.

What now? I asked myself. It seemed like nothing could top what Jesus had done these last ten days.

Half asleep, I thought about the dreams I had the week prior to this trip. The first had come to pass, and I believed the second one had as well. "Team Jesus" in their ball uniforms, had orchestrated a reunion with my sister, orchestrated my dad's salvation, and his peaceful passing. The team had cleared the ball field entirely. It was a new game. Perhaps even a new season.

So, what about the third dream? An African American man? Keys? A journey?

I was too tired to think about it. I shifted a bit, and just as I started to drift off to sleep, I heard the captain's voice.

Startled, I sat up straight, opened my eyes, and blinked a few times. I fastened my seatbelt and pulled it tight across my lap as the landing gears whined.

I listened to the wheels as they lowered. The plane rocked back and forth, and before I knew it, there was a great big thud.

We had landed safely.

It was an hour-long drive from the airport to home, and it gave me even more time to think. I was definitely ready for a change.

The first thing I realized was that I desired a new work environment. I had outgrown my present position.

After settling back home, I took some time and pursued a new job. Eventually I accepted a position at a community mental health center as the lead children's therapist. I looked forward to it, excited to learn new things.

Well, that didn't last very long. Shortly after I started the job, everything changed.

I went to work one morning only to find that my boss, the director, was gone. Vanished. Poof. No two-week notice, no explanation to those of us she'd hired, just…gone.

The next day, the new director came to me and told me they were doing away with the children's department. I was asked to stay on as a general clinician.

Right after that, the physician assistant who had joined the company the same time I did, disappeared also. He was there one day and gone the next.

Obviously, something wasn't right. I just had no idea at the time what that could be.

However, God knew things weren't right at my new workplace. And He took what was happening, orchestrated a turn of events, and of course turned what Satan meant for evil ultimately into an incredible opportunity.

CHAPTER 16

WHO HAS MY KEYS?

Shortly after I started the new job, the company took on a college intern. Nancy was about to graduate with a master's degree in social work and needed "hands on" experience.

Nancy was also a believer, was African American, and her husband was a pastor.

Right about that same time, I sent away for a set of CDs by Dr. Sam Brown of Living Faith Christian Center. The title of his teaching was called "The Supernatural Church."

The four CDs that arrived in the mail changed my life forever. I heard things I'd waited years to hear, things backed by powerful scriptures, things I knew to be true about our triune God but had not heard mentioned by any other leaders.

My faith exploded. And with that explosion, came an opening in my heart for the Lord to do a new work in my life. A seed had been planted, was growing, and grabbing at my soul.

Yes, dream number three was about to unfold.

Except not the way you might think.

Nancy turned out to be a talented social worker. We had loads of discussions about clients. The depth of her insight and compassion never ceased to amaze me.

I made friends with her husband as well. Pastor Frank and I spent one whole Saturday afternoon in a coffee shop, talking about Jesus.

I thought for sure the pastor held some important "keys" for me, with regard to the Kingdom. I was certain he was "it," the messenger in my third dream.

I focused on my new friends and on daily circumstances. I woke each morning excited about the day ahead. I listened to Dr. Brown's CDs on the drive to work, and again on the way home. And I waited for "the keys."

As I listened to Dr. Brown, I grew stronger in the Lord. I began to decree things and speak aloud my requests to God in our Lord's name. I began to bind, and loose, and receive revelation from the Holy Spirit.

In the meantime, I focused on Pastor Frank. I continued to assume he was the African American man in my third dream, and joyfully anticipated some kind of profound wisdom I was certain he had for me.

And while I focused on the pastor, Jesus continued to

prepare me for His Kingdom keys. Without a doubt, my faith was exploding.

But not through Pastor Frank.

You see, I had failed to notice that Dr. Brown is also African American.

~~~

"And I will give you the keys of the Kingdom of heaven, and whatever you bind on earth will be bound in heaven, and whatever you loose on earth will be loosed in heaven" (Matthew 16:19 NKJV).

This new season was a turning point for me. I learned to receive God's extraordinary love for me, caring less and less what others might think.

I felt happy. At least I did until once again, there was an unexpected turn of events.

Nancy came to me one morning in tears. She told me that Pastor Frank had been diagnosed with prostate cancer. They were moving to Indiana to be with his extended family.

The news shook me to the core. Even though, over the years, the Lord had repeatedly sent me people in all kinds of pain, I was still taken aback when I heard it.

Once again people I cared about were leaving with broken hearts. I was outraged at the attack on my friends. It hurt my heart that Satan had hurt theirs. I also felt confused. I had been so sure that Pastor Frank was the man in my third dream.

I was also still fairly oblivious to the changes occurring inside me as a result of Dr. Brown's CD's. All I knew was that I was supposed to take authority, speak to the nasty cancer, bind it up, and loose the light of God into Pastor Frank. I interceded for my friends when they felt weary, and repeatedly decreed that by Jesus' stripes, Frank was healed.

Though he received medical treatment and responded well to the wisdom of doctors and many prayers of friends and family, it was a time of unforeseen change.

Nancy withdrew from everyone, including me.

A mixture of feelings swirled inside all of us, always close to the surface.

While my faith was stronger and deeper than ever before, this attack of the enemy definitely caused feelings of fear, sometimes just as strong as my faith.

Looking back, I can see how the pain of it all, not knowing what would happen, and the thought of moving, was too much for Nancy to grasp during that time. And as much as I understood it, I felt a tremendous loss and sense of helplessness when she withdrew.

My friends moved within a year. I kept in touch with them for a while, until once again life took us all in different directions.

However, the last I heard, Pastor Frank was doing very well. Praise Jesus!

CHAPTER 17

LIES, LIES, EVERYWHERE LIES

I felt the need for a break, so I took a vacation from work. I should have known while I was resting, the Holy Spirit was working.

Long walks, cool April breezes that tousled my hair, horses grazing in nearby pastures, and chocolate waiting on the kitchen counter; after seven wonderful days my heart felt lighter.

I returned to work relaxed, though not necessarily eager. After I sat down at my desk, it felt as though I had never left.

I fired up my computer and sipped some coffee. I sighed as I waded through more than one hundred emails. Then I began to pull up some individual client files to refresh my memory about them. I had almost one hundred people on my caseload.

I looked at files, and at first nothing seemed unusual. However, as I kept reviewing my case notes, I noticed that every so often there was an account of actions and billable services unfamiliar to me. They were supposedly signed with my electronic signature.

Except I couldn't have provided those services or signed any case notes. I had been on vacation.

The Holy Spirit had revealed to me what appeared to be Medicaid fraud.

After the initial shock of this discovery subsided, I said a quick prayer. Then I decided it was best to follow office protocol. I went to my boss, the agency director, and met with her one on one.

She lied to my face. So, I prayed again, and not long after that, the Lord exposed her lie.

By this time, my boss was feeling quite fearful and pressured. She tried to find things about my work that warranted a reprimand. I suppose she was hoping the stress would cause me to quit.

However, I didn't feel intimidated as much as stunned by her behavior.

By law, I was a mandated reporter. That meant that while dodging her unexpected attacks, I was required to notify Medicaid about what had happened. Once I did that, no doubt my job would be over.

I felt overwhelmed by what was happening, and very uncomfortable at the thought of soon being out of work. But by the grace of God, I picked up the phone anyway. Despite my heart that pounded against my chest, I dialed the Medicaid Fraud and Abuse Hotline. I made a formal report. Then I also called our state licensure board and spoke with the executive director.

After that, I went back to my boss and sat with her, face to face. I let her know what had been done. I informed her that she was welcome to respond in whatever way she wanted, however it would not change the fact that she had used my name fraudulently and tried to lie about it.

Then... I resigned.

It didn't take long for shock to turn to rage inside of me. I wanted to sue. With everything in me, I wanted to call a lawyer, sue my boss, and sue the company.

I wanted justice. I was so disgusted, I wanted to vomit.

But instead, I squawked to everyone I knew until the burning anger inside of me subsided.

I applied for state unemployment compensation and was denied. I was told they do not assist people who resign from a job. I needed to be fired to receive help. I was offered the option of writing an appeal. Great.

Though it all seemed cockeyed to me, not to mention unfair, I wrote to the Arizona Department of Economic Security and submitted documents as an appeal of their decision. Then I found scripture after scripture about God as our avenger, and I prayed out loud.

"Beloved, do not avenge yourselves, but rather give place to wrath; for it is written, 'Vengeance is Mine, I will repay,'says the Lord"
(Romans 12:19 NKJV).

*"The L*ORD *will fight for you, and you shall hold your peace"*
(Exodus 14:14 NKJV).

Eventually, I began to heal. Though I must admit, forgiveness did not come easily.

On my knees one evening, I asked the Lord for his help.

It seemed like overnight, COVID 19 had changed life as we all once knew it. It only added to the spirit of mistrust and depression trying to choke any joy right out of me.

Forced to wear a face mask at the grocery store, the loss of goods and services, sudden deaths; it all caused me to stop, think, and dig deep into my heart about the way I had been living.

Weary from the enemy's attempts to frighten everyone, I realized I needed a deeper truth.

I disengaged from relationships that I felt required me to be someone I wasn't and did my best to speak the truth in love. I confronted issues with so-called friends and family members that I had let slide in the past.

I squared up. I focused upon forgiveness in every area of my life: asking for it, giving it, and letting go when none was needed.

And one day, as I browsed through emails and read devotionals on my computer, I noticed that for the first time ever, Living Faith Christian Center, Dr. Samuel Brown's church, was offering their School of Ministry virtually!

CHAPTER 18

INSANITY ABOUNDS

I wasted no time. As soon as I saw the notice, I started typing. I composed a brief email of inquiry and sent it to Dr. Brown's church. I simply asked if someone would be kind enough to respond to me about the School of Ministry program.

I clicked "send" on my computer, not expecting much. It was my experience that emails can easily get lost in the communication shuffle at large churches. I figured I'd probably have to follow up the email with a phone call.

That's why it surprised me when the dean of students, Dr. Houston, called me two days later. We talked, and within a week I was enrolled in school, joining others at online orientation. Praise Jesus!

Inside of ten days, a third African American man, the Dean of Students at the Living Faith Christian Center School of Ministry, invited me to take a journey with him.

And buried deep within Dr. Houston's invitation, were more keys than I could ever imagine. I was about to discover aspects of myself I did not know were there, keys to more of Jesus, and keys to Kingdom-living for the rest of my life. These keys would open the doors to that deeper truth I was seeking.

Much like the characters in a C.S. Lewis book, I felt like I had just stepped through a wardrobe into a dream.

Well, I had. Dream number three.

It seemed like school barely started when it was time to think about graduation. Ten months flashed by so quickly, I could hardly catch my breath.

I loved school. Acceptance into the fivefold ministry added a long-awaited dimension to each day. I was now living my life in technicolor.

As I became more knowledgeable in my walk with Jesus, I received a steady stream of texts and phone calls from people who were ill or wanted prayer. That hadn't changed. If anything, it had increased.

I was approached by strangers at the grocery who stopped to explain their illnesses to me. I even received requests for deliverance. Friends and ministers I hadn't heard from in years contacted me. Each wanted prayer and/or healing.

But what really caught my attention was that every day, in my home in Arizona, I would read or hear a scripture, or pray about an issue. And at the very next online church service or Bible study, Dr. Brown would specifically talk about that very same scripture or issue.

Huh? Why was God revealing to me ahead of time what my leader was going to talk about?

While I was grateful to the Lord for everything, especially for confirmation of where He wanted me to be in life, the weekly occurrences disturbed me.

But I pretended otherwise. I denied to myself that I still felt uncomfortable about letting others know just how very prophetic my life has been. I told no one.

Deep down in my heart, I was still afraid. I hardly knew the dean of the school, the teachers, or my classmates. Because of COVID, my experience was virtual. Not only that, I discovered over time that I was also the only Caucasian person in the program. Who was going to believe I knew what Dr. Brown was going to say to thousands of people before he said it?

The gifts of Spirit had followed me to ministry school. What now?

I didn't know what to do. So, I concentrated on simple tasks. I prayed, worked, and studied.

I humbly tried to blend into class time as best I could, but that proved futile. I don't believe it's ever been God's plan that I blend.

If anything, the gifts He'd given me grew stronger.

So, I told myself that no one really cared, and I didn't talk about it with anyone.

Meanwhile, I prayed and prayed for an open door to ministry, though I was frightened all over again of myself and the depth of God's calling. After all, I was just a student in the midst of seasoned, knowledgeable leaders for God.

Without even realizing it, an insidious veil of denial took over and ruled my life. Unknowingly, I was blinded by fear.

Clearly, I would ask, "Father, please bless me with work as your minister, for your glory. In the name of Jesus. Amen."

And He would answer. That is, Dr. Brown would do a teaching on a scripture I had just read two days prior. Then the phone would ring. Someone wanted healing.

So, I would pray again. "Father, please open the door and bless me with work as your minister, for your glory. In the name of Jesus. Amen."

And guess what would happen?

Like a hamster on a wheel, I kept going round and round.

I told myself I was waiting for God to open doors for me. I believed I was waiting for Him.

Except God was waiting for me.

CHAPTER 19

A Soft Landing

Obviously, I was hanging onto beliefs in my heart that weren't true for me anymore.

I danced all around the problem. I thought it was simply a matter of not allowing the opinions of others to overshadow God's gifts for me.

I could easily do that, right?

Of course, it went deeper than that. Even after all this time, I just couldn't believe that God loved me enough to share His mysteries with me or grant me foreknowledge that could help or heal a great many people.

The hamster on the wheel was just a front for feelings of unworthiness that had a hold on my heart.

Time went by, and the days chipped away at my shallow attempts to act on the Word, like the way a craftsman chips away at a hunk of wood.

Every day I'd wake and ask the Lord why I wasn't moving on into a ministry position, or why the vision He'd given me was not coming to pass.

I felt stuck and didn't like it.

Well, Jesus clearly didn't like it either. He kept speaking to me, louder and louder in my heart, until finally I couldn't deny Him.

Clearly, I was missing the mark. There are no mistakes in the Kingdom. If God's Word says we are worthy because of our Lord, then we are worthy. Period.

> *"For He made Him who knew no sin to be sin for us,*
> *that we might become the righteousness of God*
> *in Him" (2 Cor. 5:21 NKJV).*

Eventually I tired myself out, going round and round on that hamster's wheel, telling myself the same lies over and over.

I wish I could tell you that during this time I had a sudden, grand awakening that made everything right all at once.

But I didn't.

I just got so sick of myself; I couldn't stand it.

Finally, I reminded myself of the definition of insanity: doing the same thing over and over, and each time expecting different results.

So, I stopped. Thank God.

I vowed out loud to Him that the next time I talked to the Dean of the School of Ministry, I would share with him the truth of God's gifts in my life.

One morning not long after that I woke and looked around me. Sunlight blasted without apology right through the curtains on my window.

I sat up and moved to the side of the bed. Quickly I stuck my feet into my baby blue, furry slippers, and grabbed the plush throw off the bed.

Wrapping myself up, I walked the few steps over to the curtains, and peeled them back for a peek. There wasn't a cloud in the sky.

Looking out into the sun, out at the ground preparing to yield again to another planting season, I realized what a fool I'd been.

I wouldn't have been surprised if Jesus had been insulted by the way I'd allowed pride and impatience to cover over fear.

I hadn't trusted Him at all. I said all the right words and did all the right things, but deep in my heart, I had not believed.

That definitely needed to change.

So, each morning I began to confess out loud, with a grateful heart, my worthiness in Jesus. It was a powerful start.

No, there wasn't any loud clap of thunder or great big cloudburst of insight.

Instead, I changed my mind, and healing came softly.

There's something about the rural outdoors that calms me like nothing else. It's as big a part of me as every breath.

When I'm walking down country roads, whether it's a moody sky, or a breezy day, no matter, I automatically take to it like a duck takes to water. I become a part of the miracles all around me. Especially in the spring.

Butterflies, blue jays, a baby rabbit who scampers across the field while a red tail hawk eyes him from up above; when I'm out and about, it's as though I slip on the beauty of it all as easily as Cinderella did the glass slipper.

On this particular day, the sun looked down on me from behind puffy white clouds.

Passing by a field of horses, I gazed at their magnificence.

They are such beautiful creatures. I smiled at them from the road. I was certain they could see me and were smiling back.

I walked along with an unusual sense of peace inside. I sang a song to Jesus and prayed for a few minutes.

Then I looked up and followed the trail of a robin who sat on the telephone wire on my right, then flew to the maple tree at the house two doors down, then back to the phone wire.

And that's when it happened.

CHAPTER 20

HEAVEN INVADES MY MAILBOX

Jesus began to talk to me, then He talked to me some more, and then He talked to me some more, until finally, I was ready to receive what he had to say.

It's amazing how far we can see with our heart if we allow it.

I was better than okay. I was safely cocooned in gentleness and kindness, now mine for the taking. At the same time, I was filled with gentleness and kindness. I became those things, also mine for the taking.

As that revelation came to me, it also dawned on me I was experiencing Jesus' worthiness.

Wow. No more competition. No more thoughts about what ministry should look like. No more looking to others for acceptance. No more pretending.

Most importantly, I felt no fear.

The Lord was revealing Himself to me.

Finally, I understood.

As a believer, it was never meant for me to figure out on my own, how to live in this world. It is meant for all of those of us to simply believe, to keep our eyes on Jesus and co-create with our Father, God.

Proverbs tells us to lean on the Lord's understanding, and not our own. Thank goodness for that.

> *"Trust in the Lord with all your heart And lean not on your own understanding; In all your ways acknowledge Him, And He shall direct your paths"*
> *(Proverbs 3:5-6).*

Graduation from the School of Ministry finally came and just as quickly, passed. The leaves on the trees turned colors, the morning air crisp, and before I knew it the holidays had whizzed right by.

Once again, it was spring. I thought it would never come.

I was entertaining family from out of town, taking a break from my normal routine.

The afternoon sun looked so inviting, I decided to walk to the mailbox.

As I approached the end of the drive, I took a mental inventory of the fridge. Did I need to go to the grocery today? What should I make for dinner?

I pulled down the squeaky mailbox door, stuck my hand into

the metal hut, and retrieved a pile of envelopes. Expecting a bunch of junk mail, I stood and began shuffling.

"Oh my gosh!" I cried out to no one.

My jaw dropped as I stopped and stared at the square envelope looking up at me.

There, in front of me, was an official letter from the Arizona Department of Economic Security. Among other things, they manage Medicaid contracts.

Almost two years had passed since my previous employer had tried to engage me in her schemes. Seeing the envelope instantly took me back. My nervous system sounded a silent alarm.

Curious as well as anxious, I stood still. I raised my head and looked around. The sun peeked through a sky full of scattered clouds. It reassured me that all was well.

I took a deep breath, let it out, and with shaky fingers I opened the letter and read it out loud.

When I was done, I gasped all over again. My hand flew to my heart, and after a few seconds, I read the letter out loud again.

I wanted to be sure it said what I thought it said.

After all this time the Arizona Department of Economic Security had found my last employer to be "in error." Not only that, but also enclosed was a check, offered to me as the restitution of state unemployment wages.

I almost fainted.

I stood at the mailbox for a minute longer and it suddenly struck me how much knowing Jesus had changed my life.

I had grown from feeling afraid of His mysterious, miraculous ways, to living each day expecting them, and leaning on His presence with every breath.

And in every breath, I experienced His peace. I lived hand in hand with the incredible creativity that is the essence of obedience to God's Word.

On that day, He had presented to me yet another key to the Kingdom, another glimpse of a perfect love so vast, I've yet to comprehend it.

What happened showed me that the blessings encapsulated in Jesus' faithfulness to our Father, given freely to all those who believe, are more powerful than anything on earth.

No court system, no amount of money, nothing could have eased my heart or taken away the pain of what had happened the incredible way the Lord had.

Heaven had invaded earth and stuck the outcome of the battle in my mailbox.

Jesus had heard my prayers and gone before our Father…on my behalf!

Humble tears spilled from my eyes. Stunned and excited, I let them dance their way down my cheeks as once again, God left me standing, speechless.

I felt free of the world's expectations, way deep down in my heart. All of me was free, and it was all because of Jesus.

CHAPTER 21

Something in the Air

After that day at the mailbox, I finally understood what it means to enter into rest with the Lord. My faith took such a giant leap, I didn't feel the need to try and make anything happen anymore. Instead, I began the journey of walking in the perfect love that is God.

I took comfort in the routine of household chores, a miracle in and of itself. I came to enjoy the tasks of everyday life. I let long walks and long talks with Jesus fill me up.

Miracles continued to follow me just about everywhere I went. My understanding of our triune God deepened, as He gave me new knowledge and revelation. I learned about the healing Jesus gave at the cross to those who believe. He showed me how it includes everything about us. He didn't just heal our bodies, but also our hearts, the way we think, and our souls.

I woke each morning excited about the day. The Lord's peace

inside me grew, and as fear seemed to dwindle.

For the most part I felt joy, except I must admit that way down deep, I also felt a very subtle, nagging sense of unease.

Almost daily I detected a teeny, tiny, almost tangible thread of tension in the air. I couldn't help but wonder if the stinking vapor of death caused by COVID 19 wanted to linger.

Dear Readers, I pray that by now, the words I've put to paper have somehow added to your life.

I don't care to regurgitate to you the details of COVID19 or talk about the mess of things that constitutes the six o'clock news.

I want you to know love. I want to show you the other side of fear that comes with embracing almighty God in His entirety.

Looking back, it would have been easy for me to simply write a small pamphlet and quote a scripture that says God is good (which He is). But that would not do anyone, least of all our Lord, justice.

Or I could say to you, "Believe in Jesus, fear not, and have faith. God bless you. Write to me and I will pray for you."

Well, that's simple, if not cliché. While prayer is certainly powerfully important, it's a far cry from a revelation of the other side of fear.

Instead, I've hoped to show you who you are in Jesus, the way you've been created. By sharing with you firsthand all that God,

Jesus, and the Holy Spirit have done in my life, I pray you won't be frightened of your own. God is good. He cares about you.

I have purposely revealed to you a life filled with phenomenal experiences. I pray you might feel inspired, and excited to honor God's written Word, and experience heaven on earth,

I want everyone to know the truth about our triune God and the good news of His Kingdom.

Anything worth having requires courage, brains, and heart. The journey to the other side of fear is no exception. It brings to mind the yellow brick road in L. Frank Baum's The Wizard of Oz.

Are there lions and tigers and bears on this road?

You bet. They are disguised as lies, deceit, perversity, and lack of accountability.

However, don't forget you are protected on this adventure. And while you may not be wearing shiny ruby shoes, you have with you the truth of the living Word, the greatest weapon that exists.

Did you know, too, that if you believe steadfastly, if you do not allow your faith to waver, if you trust in our triune God, you are able to do all that Jesus did and more?

*"Most assuredly, I say to you, he who believes in Me,
the works that I do he will do also; and greater works
than these he will do, because I go to My Father"
(John 14:12 NKJV).*

And in the book of Matthew Jesus says:

*"As you go, proclaim this message: 'The kingdom of
heaven has come near.' Heal The sick, raise
the dead, cleanse those who have leprosy, drive
out demons. Freely You have received; freely give"
(Matthew 10:7-8 NKJV).*

My friends, as far as I know, Jesus hasn't changed.
Nor has His mandate.

CHAPTER 22

A Miraculous Life

I just want to get out of here.

I couldn't help it. Some people enjoy shopping, but I'm not one of them. Standing in a long line at a Walmart checkout aisle was about as far away from a good time as I could get.

I yawned. Then, I turned around to look at something besides the back of the person in line in front of me.

"Oh, hi!" Standing right behind me was a woman I used to see every Sunday, during the time I'd attended church.

What was her name? Kate? No. Catherine? Yes!

Delighted to have remembered her name, I smiled. "How are you?"

Catherine looked at me, then glanced down at the floor for a second. With creased brows, she began, "Not so great. I had an eye appointment last week, and the doctor says I have macular degeneration in my left eye."

"Oh my gosh!"

The words no sooner left my mouth, when the Holy Spirit clearly told me to pray for this woman's healing.

"Catherine, would you mind if I said a quick prayer?"

"No. Not at all. Please!"

So right there in the middle of Walmart, I gently took Catherine's hands and called upon God. I bound up macular degeneration and all evil spirits of affliction. Then I asked that He manifest His healing in her and restore her eyesight to perfect vision.

Right about that time, it became my turn to check out.

I reached into my cart and laid my items, one by one, on the conveyor belt. Then I turned to say goodbye to Catherine.

"Take good care. Let me know what happens."

"Sure." Catherine smiled. "Thank you!"

The cashier totaled my purchase.

Eager to leave, I picked up my plastic bags and all but sprinted out of the Supercenter. Grateful to be out of there and anxious to get home, I forgot all about Catherine.

When the following Sunday came, I noticed she wasn't at church.

Since we usually didn't socialize beyond a "hello," I didn't think much of it.

After the service I went home and prepared for a busy week. Work, chores, company coming next Friday evening, I realized I'd better go to the grocery that afternoon or nothing else would get done that week.

I groaned. Standing in line at the grocery store is about as much fun for me as standing at the checkout at Walmart.

Once again, I yawned. With two people ahead of me, my foot on the bottom rung of the cart, I turned to look around. And there she was again. Catherine was in line at the grocery, three people behind me.

"Catherine!" I stuck my head out to the side of the line and waved to her.

"Oh my gosh! Barb, wait up for me!"

Twenty minutes later we stood at the grocery exit.

"My granddaughter didn't feel well this morning, so I skipped church to help out her mom. But I wanted to tell you. I can't believe I ran into you again. Barb, it's gone!"

"What?"

"My eyes! I saw the doctor again, and there's no degeneration! None!"

Catherine's smile was as big as Texas. I half expected her to dance right there in the grocery store. I know I was tempted, myself.

"Wow, Catherine! Praise Jesus!"

Passersby looked over at me. Most of them smiled as I gave my friend a great big hug.

Catherine and I talked briefly for a moment. She mentioned

she would let the pastor at church know about the healing. Then we said our goodbyes.

What happened with Catherine is just one of many instances where the Lord has honored me and used me to bless someone with a miracle.

For instance, one time a woman came to see me, distraught and in tears. Her pregnant daughter had been told by a doctor that her unborn child, if born, would more than likely never grow or function normally. The doctor had advised the young, pregnant mother to abort her baby.

I listened to Grandma and helped her calm down. Then we prayed. I decreed, and she agreed, that the next ultrasound would show her daughter's baby normal and healthy.

And it did. Praise Jesus!

Another time, not long ago, a doctor told me I had skin cancer on my face. She scheduled outpatient surgery for me to have the cells removed.

I was shocked. I went home and prayed, outraged at what I consider an affliction of the enemy.

I stood in front of the bathroom mirror, touched my face and adamantly decreed God's healing.

On the day of outpatient surgery, I waited calmly for the surgeon to arrive. And when he did, I asked if he would please examine my face again, before cutting it up.

I vividly recall the way the doctor came close, bent down, and looked through a small magnifying glass at my skin. Then he straightened, stepped back about three feet, and crossed his arms over his chest. He looked at me and said, "This is healed. There's nothing wrong."

I just smiled, along with the young assistant wearing a cross around her neck. Quietly I replied, "I know. Praise Jesus!"

Our Lord is true to His Word. As a believer, He has honored me with the gift of doing things that He did while on earth. Of course, it's Him doing it through me. I'm simply the vessel.

All glory to God! Being used so that others might receive His healing, is just one piece of the multifaceted journey to the other side of fear. The more I have learned to trust in His mysterious ways, the more He keeps inviting me to be part of them.

Remember, Jesus says if we believe steadfastly, we will not only do what He did, we will do more.

CHAPTER 23

CALLING ALL INTERCESSORS

I don't exactly understand why, but it seems that in general, gifts of prophecy haven't been talked about much in churches, at least not in the ones I've attended. Yet the apostle Paul wrote:

> **"Pursue love, and desire spiritual gifts, but especially that you may prophesy"**
> **(1 Cor. 14:1 NKJV).**

Hmm, if no one mentions this particular gift, how will we, the body of Christ, be able to recognize it, let alone do it?

And if we do recognize it, are we supposed to keep quiet about it? It seems to be the way, at least until recently.

As I walked down the narrow road, I couldn't have asked for a more beautiful afternoon.

I had a lot to talk over with Jesus. Attending a school of ministry had caused me to think back now and then, often resulting in new perspective.

My thoughts wandered back to Pastor Johnson, the pastor of the small church I had once attended. Though I hadn't seen the pastor in years, he weighed noticeably heavy on my heart that day.

Wondering what that was all about, I went to the Lord. "Why am I thinking of Him, Jesus?"

"Pray for him." There was no mistaking what the quiet voice inside me said.

So, taking my time, I passed by the donkey across the street and the chickens around the corner, while I prayed out loud for the pastor. And I no sooner finished and barely uttered "Amen'," when a shiny, silver, Dodge pickup pulled up beside me.

The truck stopped, and Pastor Johnson, himself, leaned out the driver's window!

"Hi Barbara," he smiled.

Needless to say, I was stunned. The Holy Spirit was blatantly orchestrating this encounter and I had no clue why. I stared blankly at the pastor. I could barely say hello back. The first thing I did after years apart, was babble to the man.

"I just prayed for you." With a crease between my eyes, I tried my best to smile.

Pastor Johnson chuckled. "Good! I need it! Everything okay?"

"Um, yeah."

"Okay. Good to see you, Barbara. Take care."

Then the pastor drove off. Just like that.

Bewildered, I stood at the side of the road and stared as the pickup moved on, leaving me behind in a cloud of dust.

Pastor Johnson had faded away just as quickly as he'd come.

"Lord, what just happened?"

Shaking my head and speaking out loud, I resumed my walk.

And I forgot all about the encounter, that is, until a few months later.

The loud ring from the next room startled me.

I laid down my book, walked to the kitchen counter, and looked at my phone.

The caller ID said it was Susan.

Casually I picked it up, pressed the green button, and said hello.

"Barb, you'll never guess what happened." An anxious voice all but barked at me through the phone.

Taken aback, I held it away from my face for a second and said nothing.

Susan, on the other hand, kept right on talking.

"Pastor Johnson has been sick, Barb. It was serious. Something was wrong with his stomach. They operated twice, and twice he flatlined on the table. Thankfully though, he was revived. He's going to be okay."

Tears sprang to my eyes. Immediately, I pictured the pastor only a few months ago pulling up beside me in his silver truck.

I remembered how befuddled I felt at the time.

Wow. For a second, I didn't know what to say to Susan. Totally taken by surprise, I was at first, overcome with gratefulness to Jesus that the pastor was okay.

Quietly I thanked my friend for calling and set the phone back down on the counter. I took a minute and said another prayer of thanks to God, in my King's name.

And then it hit me. The Lord had trusted me enough to ask me to prophetically pray for the safety of Pastor Johnson. Holy Spirit God inside me knew what was to come and had obviously prompted me to intercede for this man.

Though it wasn't the first time this had happened, I was every bit as awestruck and humbled as if it had been.

It appears as though another reason to journey to the other side of fear, another reason to be comfortable with all of God's miraculous, supernatural ways, is so He can use us ahead of time to get in death's way and perhaps save someone's life.

CHAPTER 24

The Price of Eggs

As you travel the road to a miraculous, astounding life with our triune God, there's something I'd like to share.

In the book of John, chapter 17, you will find that Jesus prayed to our Father before going to the cross. Here's some of what He said:

> **"And now, O Father, glorify Me together with Yourself, with the glory which I had with You before the world was"**
> **(John 17:5 NKJV).**

What's that? What did the Lord just say?

Did Jesus just say He shared God's glory, together with God, before the world was created? Isn't He asking to be glorified with our Father once again, back at that time?

As believers, the Lord tells us He left with us the Holy Spirit, a person, the third person of the Godhead, who dwells with us and in us. He is our helper. He is also a form of our triune God.

> **"*To them God willed to make known what are the riches of the glory of this* Mystery *among the Gentiles: which is Christ in you, the hope of glory"* (Col. 1:27 NKJV).**

Well, if Jesus tells us we will do what He did and more, and He's asked to be glorified back to the glory He shared with our Father before the world was, and He is in us, does that mean we will be glorified back before the world was also, along with Him?

Friends, as I've prayed about these final chapters, the depth of what this means for believers is infinite.

The journey from fear to the other side of it is the most daunting, powerful journey a person can make. And at the end of the road is glory! God's glory, the same glory that was before the foundation of the world, for us to share!

Jesus has enabled us to be with Him in the fullness of the Kingdom, to be glorified with Him and our Father. It has been done. What power there is in that! It has already happened, supernaturally, through faith.

First, it began with God's faith, the faith He used to speak the universe into creation.

Next, it is the very same faith that is Jesus' faith. Third, it is the very same measure of faith we have been given. And finally, it is the faith that the Holy Spirit uses to unite us with God, through Jesus, when we believe.

We are in Him, and He in us. Dear readers, this is literal. The other side of fear is faith in all we can't see. It is knowing we have access to the Kingdom, and to everything we will ever need while we are still here on earth.

It is also knowing that just as almighty God spoke the world into creation, we can speak things into creation, also. By speaking and decreeing His Word, by speaking Jesus into every situation, we can co-create with our heavenly Father. We walk with the power of almighty God.

By letting go of fear of the unknown, fear of a wondrous life as a believer in Jesus Christ as our Lord and Savior, we allow ourselves to receive an incredible gift. According to the book of John, we can live in the very glory of God that was there, before creation.

Most of all, we can give ourselves the miraculous gift of living on earth as it is in heaven. Right now! We can take back the Garden. We don't have to wait. We can join with our triune God and do it. Now!

And *THAT*, dear readers, is the other side of fear!

Did you know that God is love?

"He who does not love does not know God, for God is love"
(1 John 4:8 NKJV).

That means that everything you see around you, the sun, clouds, moon, stars, His whole universe was spoken into existence with love – a love so perfect and powerful, it is unfathomable.

And if we choose to believe, we can walk in that love, right here, right now.

There is nothing to fear about our miraculous, triune God. His supernatural ways in our lives are simply incredible displays of His love for us if we choose to believe.

One day not long ago, I found myself yearning for chocolate chip cookies.

Have you ever had a yearning for anything? If so, you know that such a thing is not easily assuaged. When cravings sneak up on you, they take over and trump everything else that's happening at the time.

I wanted chocolate chip cookies. I also wanted the kind made with natural ingredients. So, I considered baking them myself.

However, I was out of eggs.

Well, have you been to a grocery store lately? Farm-fresh eggs are expensive. It looked as though I would have to mortgage my house in order to afford a dozen.

I gave up the idea and went for a walk.

An hour or so later, sun-kissed, and relaxed, I slowly

meandered up the drive to my front door. I was almost there when my neighbor's screen door flew open, and Carol rushed outside.

"Barbara! Hi!" She smiled and waved as she crossed from her house to mine. "Hold up! Could you use a dozen eggs? A friend of mine has chickens and brings the eggs to me, but I can't use them right now."

Yes, God cares. He is love.

Need I say more?

CHAPTER 25

PERFECT LOVE

I'd like to return now to the night all of this began, the night the Lord brought an angel to my door.

If you recall, on that particular night I missed Michael, a loved one, and I felt extremely sad inside.

And in response, the Lord let me know He, Himself, was nearby.

That night, Jesus also confessed me before the angels of God, told me to put pen to paper, and to let all of you know you are never alone. He said that is the first step to receiving miracles.

Dear readers, I pray I have done what the Lord has asked, if not more. I pray my words have somehow added to your life. Only you can say for sure.

What I do know however, is that by choosing to listen to

Jesus, to do what He told me to do that wintry night, He has led me deeper into the greatest love story that will ever exist.

Yes, deeper, and deeper, His love keeps unraveling in my life. Thank you, my friends, for allowing me to share it with you.

I had no idea when I put pen to paper that the only way to show you that you are never alone, that in Jesus there's nothing to fear, would be to go on the journey with you. I pray that each time I've shared with you an unusual experience that's happened in my life, it has brought you closer to understanding yourself, and your own journey with our precious Lord.

I did not realize my faith and trust in my Lord had grown to the point where not only am I no longer frightened of the spiritual gifts God has for me, but I embrace them. His ways are life to those who believe.

I pray that you know, more than anything, how important they are and what blessings they are meant to be in your life, as they are in mine.

Friends, I wish there was a magic wand I could wave for you that would take away life's hurts and upsets. But there isn't. However, there is a supernatural life you've been born to know. Learning about it and becoming all that you've been created to be is the antidote to fear, the answer to whatever the struggle has been.

His name is Jesus. He is the only reason we are able to know that God is love, and experience Him in our lives now, today, on earth as it is in heaven.

Thinking back, I have been honored over the years to sit with hundreds of people, each with their own account and definition of love, if not lack of it.

I have heard countless stories of horrendous abuse, of deceit and lies, and I've also witnessed miraculous recovery and healing in people's lives. I have sat with professional people such as doctors, lawyers, pastors, as well as many people who never made it past the eighth grade.

Once upon a time my profession was my identity. And what stands out to me, as I look back, is that it never occurred to me when I first entered the counseling profession, that love would turn out to be a person. I was the blind leading the blind.

There are no accidents. As you have likely guessed by now, my time at graduate school was clearly orchestrated by God. Did I mention that the Dean of the Community Counseling program, the head of the whole department where I went to school, was a believer?

And I am grateful. Good counsel can be very helpful to people.

However, only Jesus saves.

Only love saves.

To me, there is nothing more precious than the human heart.

Show me the small, purple wildflower on the side of the road, sticking up out of the dry dirt hard as clay, and I'll show you the magnificence of my Lord, Jesus.

This is a glimpse of who He is: Good Shepherd, King of Kings, Lamb of God, Lord of Lords, Messiah, Prince of Peace, Almighty, Awesome, The Beginning, Blessed, Conqueror, Defender, Deliverer, Faithful, Forgiver, Generous, Glorious, Graceful, Hero, Judge, Kind, Loving, Never Ending, Omnipotent, Omnipresent, Pleaser, Powerful, Providing, Pure, Righteous, Victorious, Wise, Wonderful.

This is a glimpse of who you are to God: in Him you are chosen, holy, blameless, adopted as God's child, protected, anointed; you have an angel that goes before you, and a heavenly host of angels sent to minister to you according to God's Word.

Dear readers, there were warrior angels all around my house on the chilly night this book was born. They were standing guard outside, while inside my house Jesus was standing guard over my heart. Again, I pray that what He asked of me has blessed you.

If you choose to believe and travel to the other side of fear, remember that you will never be alone. There will be miracles everywhere.

Should you want prayer or encouragement, please email me at the address found at the end of this book. I would love to hear from you. Though it might take some time, I will answer you.

"The LORD bless you and keep you; The LORD make His face shine upon you, And be gracious to you;" (Numbers 6:24-26 NKJV).

EPILOGUE

The sound of the phone startled me.

Focused on editing this book, I jumped as the sing-song sound of Verizon about gave me a heart attack.

"Hello?" Mindlessly I picked up the noisy rectangle. My stomach growled as I waited for someone on the other end to start talking. Hmm…I'd forgotten that I'd missed lunch.

"Barbara?"

"Oh my gosh! Gretta?" I couldn't believe my ears. "How are you? Is everything okay?"

Memories instantly came flooding back. I could see her long blond hair covering her face as she spoke of rape and abuse. I could hear her all over again, telling me she was afraid to live, barely whispering to me that she sensed angels and demons, and thought she was crazy.

"Barbara, I'm doing great. I'm not sick anymore, and work is going well. I'm going to two Bible studies a week, plus church, and I'm praying about going to ministry school. And I'm getting ready to write a children's book! Do you think you could help me? How do I start?"

A great big smile spread across my face. Hearing the joy in Gretta's voice somehow made every single struggle I've ever had, worth it.

"Gretta, I'd be happy to help you any way I can. I'm so glad you called me. I think where I'd start, is to simply get into the habit of writing. Every day, just write something about anything you want. I'll call you in a week or two to see how it is going."

"Okay. I just wanted you to know I'm doing really well. Thank you."

Hearing those words from Gretta brought tears to my eyes. We said our goodbyes and ended the call.

Once shattered, believing lie upon lie, this woman lived in terror, the deck seemingly stacked against her.

However, our Lord knew better.

Dear readers, if you've read my words this far then perhaps you've realized I've been writing all along for you, as well as for all the "Gretta's" out there.

God bless you as you bravely go forth into the plan and potential that He has for you.

Remember: you are not alone. You are not crazy. And there's nothing to fear.

CONTACT US

beckministries5@gmail.com

First and foremost, please feel free to send me an email! I'd love to hear about you, your journey, and how I might pray for you. I am usually able to respond to emails within twenty-four hours.

As a licensed minister of the Gospel as well as a licensed professional counselor, it'd be a privilege to come and talk with you and your group about life and the truth of our miraculous Lord. No matter how big or small, I'd love to join with you. Just send a request via email.

Also, if you'd like to become a partner or make a one-time offering to this ministry, please let me know. It is your support that makes it all possible.

Thank you.
God be with you.
Barbara

BARBARA BECK